THE SILENT GENERATION

By Haig Sarajian

Dedication

To the sacred soil, skies and streams of
Historic Armenia
Whose Beauty remains Eternal
And
To the Martyrs and to the Survivors
To the Silenced and to the Silent
They were more than Victims they
Are our Heroes.

Prologue

One of my earliest memories was of my father, Avedis Sarajian, gazing at a large portrait that hung in the living room of our apartment in Brooklyn. The portrait was a reproduction of a postcard-sized black and white photo that I had seen in the family photo album. The colorized version hanging on the living room wall showed an older man of about 60, seated and wearing a fez. Seated to his right was an older woman holding an adorably chubby infant. Behind them, a pretty young woman and handsome young man gazed benignly for the camera. As my father would stare at the portrait, his eyes would fill with tears and he would walk off, unable to speak. I grew up wondering who these people were. They were never spoken of, despite their ever-presence in our lives.

Many years later, my mother, Ardemis Sarajian, told me that the older people in the picture were Dikran and Mariam Sarajian, my paternal grandparents. The young woman and child, she told me, were my father's sister and her child. The young man was a nephew, a student. He held a book that he had bought with some of the money that my father had sent back to "the Old Country" from America. But why had my father's eyes filled each time he looked at the photo? It didn't make sense.

Years after that, I learned more. I discovered that the older people in the photo were in fact my father's parents. But, the young woman with the adorable baby was not his sister, but rather, his first wife, Vartouhi. The baby was my father's first-born child, a daughter named Mariam. My father had never seen his first-born. He had left for America before she was born, hoping to earn enough money in this land of opportunity to bring his family to join him.

How would he know that fate and the Turks would intervene with his plan? The three generations of my family shown in that portrait were brutally butchered as a part of the Turkish hierarchal mandate to dispose of its entire Armenian citizenry. Almost all of the inhabitants of my father's ancestral village of Efkere in the Eastern part of Turkey were slain. This scene was reenacted a thousand fold throughout the mountains and hills of "Historic Armenia."

My name is Haig Sarajian and I am the son of two survivors of the Armenian Genocide. The following pages contain the life stories of my parents, Avedis and Ardemis. Together with my brother Dick and my sister Mary, I came to learn their stories. They did not share these stories willingly; they had to be coaxed out of them with great care. Indeed, it was not until my mother Ardemis was 80 years old that she began to share her story. During a stay at the sedate Mohonk Mountain House in New Paltz, New York, a few days after the family had gathered to celebrate her 80th birthday, my mother began to recall the old days. My sister Mary gently led mom through dates, facts, places and figures. Finally, we could discover and document the early lives of Ardemis and Avedis Sarajian. Without that history, this assembled narrative would have been impossible. My brother, sister and I have also contributed our own personal remembrances to help tie the knots to this intricate weave which completes the fabric of our parents' life story. Additionally, we have asked our cousins and other relatives to provide information where needed.

We are the children of the 20th century, but more significantly, we are the first generation to be born of the survivors of the Turkish Massacres of the Armenians in 1915. The American press at the time reported on the Ottoman Turkish "depopulation" of the Armenian subject population as a "planned extermination." The resulting slaughter affected every Armenian, from that year forward, and then forever after.

Under the guise of maintaining internal security, the Ottoman Turkish government led by the "Young Turks", Pashas Talaat, Enver and Djemal, systematically exterminated the entire Armenian nation. Only a handful of Armenians survived. The Turkish Government finally had an answer to the "Armenian Question." Their answer: the total elimination of the Armenian people.[1]

Young Armenian men were conscripted into the Turkish army and they became "instant" fatalities of the war. All other Armenian men, women and children, the very young and the very aged, the healthy and the infirmed, were ordered to assemble in their village squares and were marched into oblivion. No villyet, village, town or city was exempt. More than two million Armenians were forcibly uprooted from their ancestral homes and most became statistics in the 20th century's first genocide.

It is estimated that one and one-half million Armenians perished in the hills and plains, deserts and rivers of the ancient lands of historic Armenia. The world silently watched. In time, it spoke in unknowing but derisive tonality of the "Starving Armenians." What a hateful, but telling description. In all, it was a shameful reaction to a sardonic act. The civilized conscience of the world came to regret its lack of intervention. The seeds of future genocide had been sown. Those Armenians who miraculously escaped scattered throughout the world. These brave and select few begot the generation of which I am proud to be a part.

Presently, precious few of this heroic generation, the eye-witnesses of these unimaginable horrors remain alive. Most alive now were only babies 94 years ago, and time and sorrow have dimmed their memories. Their tears have dried and their sobs have silenced. Most of their beloved brothers and sisters have found their final sanctuary in the graveyards of the Diaspora.

But, even decades ago, our parents and grandparents rarely spoke of these horrors. When they did, it was done privately and in whispers, and only amongst each other. As a youngster, I often wondered why. Was it a "grownups' secret?" What had happened? What was this "Akhzor" and "Chardt"? Later, when I was a young adult and had some knowledge of our history, I rationalized that our parents just wanted to forget those terrible days. They certainly did not want to burden their young children with tales of wholesale bloodshed that haunted their own lives.

Today, I think that to be true, but I also believe that they felt a gnawing and consuming guilt. Why should they have survived, while a whole nation died? That millstone of their remorse must have weighed heavily on them as they struggled to continue on. For me and my peers, the one constant was pain and anguish etched in their faces and mirrored in their eyes. Yet, as dead as their eyes looked, this was always a silent generation, and seldom did they reveal the terrors of the past.

In 1998, in an effort to better understand the memories recalled herein, my wife Mary and I traveled to the "Homeland", the birthplaces of each of our parents. This Pilgrimage led by Armen Aroyan was an opportunity for Mary and me, together with other children and grandchildren of Survivors, to visit Historic Armenia- the interior of Eastern Turkey, Anatolia. The group always paused and paid homage in those very villages in which we were individually rooted. I saw and stood in the villages of Efkere, the birthplace of my father, and Shabin Karahisar, the birthplace of my mother. I shuddered with emotion as we drove through the beautiful countryside and approached each picturesque village, each flowing spring and well. My heart leapt with joy beholding the natural beauty and glory of our ancestral homeland.

This was the "Yergeer," (homeland) of our parents. I was, time and time again, overwhelmed that I was really here, on the sacred soil of my people. My roots. But soon my tears of joy turned to tears of profound sadness. We walked the pathways of each village and sought the ruins of every church. In each village, we bowed our heads in prayer and said our "Hoki-Hankist" (prayers for the souls of the deceased). For this land was also the graveyard of millions of our murdered people; the site of misery, sickness and torture for many others. Our spiritual leader, Archbishop Mesrop Ashjian, implored and beseeched our Creator to finally grant peace to our martyred dead. We wept, overcome with visions of what were the ravages of 1915. Together, we united in body, mind and spirit and memorialized the supreme and ultimate sacrifice of our forbearers, as we solemnly sang Hayr Mer (The Lord's Prayer.)

This time in my homeland permitted me to bridge my past in new and intimate ways. If this was not "closure", the experience would at least grant me and my fellow travelers the grace to grieve with some measure of peace and solace. I share the memories herein in an attempt to personalize and preserve the lives and struggles of my parents, Avedis and Ardemis. I feel the retelling of their stories is my responsibility. Indeed, it is my privilege to pass their stories on to the generations yet to come, whose veins will pulsate with the same blood as our parents: this is their inheritance.

We, the first generation of the Diaspora, have been entrusted with the tales of their times. We are their storytellers, their historians, and their biographers. Sadly, many of this brave generation have chosen to live silently, perhaps even secretively, to bury their personal history along with their bodies. I have spent the time compiling this history so that the story of my parents will not be forgotten. I remember them with love and passion. My parents and their compatriots were more than survivors, more than victims. They were, and are, the ultimate victors over evil. They were, in fact, conquerors. They faced in mortal combat the First Genocide of the Twentieth Century. They overcame the savagery of the Turks and their insidious plot to eliminate all Armenians. They lived!

Contents

If they to ask me where one can meet the most miracles on this planet of ours, I would name Armenia first of all…"
Rockwell Kent, nineteenth century American painter

Chapter 1

Avedis Sarajian: His Family

A vedis Sarajian, my father, was born on October 16, 1890 in the village of Efkere, Turkey. Efkere is a small hillside town, twelve miles northeast of the major Anatolian city of Gesarya (also called Kayseri, population 400,000), in central Turkey. Avedis was the youngest of three children. His mother's name was Mariam (nee Kaloostian). Mariam was born in the village of Nirze, a neighboring village to Efkere, probably in the mid 1860s. Her father's name was Mgrditch and her mother's name with Eghisabet (nee Kederian). Avedis' father's name was Dikran, and he was born

1

in the early 1860s in Efkere. Dikran's parents' names were Asadoor and Goulana (nee Keosaian). Unfortunately we have no further knowledge or information regarding any of Avedis' grandparents.

Family lore leads to the conclusion that the Sarajians were longtime residents of Efkere. Dikran and Mariam were married in the early 1880s. Avedis' sister, Makrouhi, the eldest of Dikran and Mariam's children, was born in the early 1880s. She married around the turn of the century and lived in Efkere with her husband, (unknown first name) Keleshian. At the time of the Genocide in 1915, Makrouhi had five living children. A photograph of one of her sons is the sole record we have of her family. Her youngest son was included in the portrait I described earlier. The boy's name, and his siblings' names, sadly remain unknown. Minas, Avedis' older brother, was born in the 1880s. Minas was married as well but his wife's name and the names of their two children are unknown.

All of the Sarajians most likely lived in close proximity to Soorp Stepanos Church. Dikran and Mariam's home was constructed of cut stone blocks quarried from a local mountain. The house was nestled on a hillside a few hundred yards from the church, in West Efkere. The house was located in front of the church, downhill and to the North of the Church.[2] Soorp Stepanos was, and still is, the tallest structure in Efkere.

Chapter 2

Ardemis Sergenian: Her Family

On May 15, 1902, twelve years after my father Avedis Sarajian was born, my mother Ardemis Sergenian came into the world. Ardemis was born in the mountainous village of Shabin Karahisar in North Central Turkey. She was the fifth of six children born to Sarkis and Anna Papazian Sergenian. Sarkis Sergenian wed Anna Papazian in Shabin Karahisar, Turkey, in the 1890s. Ardemis had two older brothers, Andon and Kaloust and two older sisters, Victoria and Aghavni. The youngest in the family was Ardemis' baby brother, Souren.

A. Ardemis' Father Sarkis' Family

Ardemis' father Sarkis was born in Shabin Karahisar in the late 1860s. Family lore hints that the Sergenians migrated to Shabin Karahisar from an area near the ancient Eastern Armenian city of Ani. Sarkis' parents were named Mgrditch and Serpouhi. Little else is known about them.

Sarkis' parents had two older children, both girls. One girl was married to an Ozanian, very likely related to the family of the famed Armenian hero, General Antranik Ozanian. The second of the Mgrditch Sergenian girls was married to a man named Hususian. The Hususian family was another family renowned in the annals of Karahisartsi freedom fighters. The Turks killed both Sergenian girls and their husbands and children in 1915. Sarkis also had a first cousin one generation removed whose name was Nishan Sergenian. Later in this account we will delve a bit deeper into the life and family of cousin Nishan.

B. Ardemis' Mother Anna's Family

Anna was the third of five children. She was the born around 1870 in the city of Tokat, a fairly large town near Sepastia. Her father was Mgrditch Papazian but again we unfortunately have no record concerning his wife (Anna's mother) other than that she was an Armenian girl from Tokat.

The eldest of the Papazian children was Dikran. Anna's older sister was Hripsimeh who was married to an Odabashian. Anna's two younger sisters were Dourig (married name unknown) and Haiganoush who was married to a Mozian. My mother's cousin and fellow survivor, Seranoush Agababian, was the daughter of Haiganoush Mozian. Seranoush's two sons are Haig and Edward Agababian, our second cousins. Haig died a few years ago in Boston, Massachusetts.

The Papazians (my great grandparents) were long-time residents of Tokat, which is located 75-100 miles west of Shabin Karahisar, and close to the provincial capital of Sivas (Sepasastia). Mgrditch, who was born in the 1840s, was a professional who was trained in engineering and construction. We believe that his wife died shortly after the birth of their last child, Haiganoush, sometime in the 1870s.

According to Ardemis' recollections, in the mid or late 1870s, Mgrditch was commissioned to work on an engineering project in Jerusalem. He lived and worked in this ancient city for some period of time. His wife and children accompanied him to the Holy Land. We know that Anna (Ardemis' mother) was known as a "Haji", one who has made the pilgrimage to Jerusalem.

Apparently, Mgrditch's work involved building or repairing the aqueducts of Jerusalem. When his work was completed, Mgrditch returned to Turkey, but not to Tokat. His wife had died and Mgrditch abandoned his ancestral home (because of his wife's death?) and instead settled in Shabin

Karahisar. We believe that at this time Mgrditch was a widower with five young children (one of whom was Anna, Ardemis' mother.)

A short time after arriving in Karahisar, a beautiful village with a Roman Fortress atop its mount (the "Pert"), Mgrditch courted and married Nazeli Ozanian, the raucous and boisterous older sister and surrogate mother of the young Antranik Ozanian, the future Armenian hero. Nazeli became Anna's step-mother.

I remember my mother Ardemis recalling her mother Anna's tales about the young Antranik. The energetic teenager, at least for a short time, lived and played in the Papazian household. Sometime around 1890, after running afoul of the local Turkish police, Antranik Ozanian left Shabin Karahisar, never again to see his birthplace. The legendary Armenian hero went to Constantinople, and eventually into everlasting fame, fighting for his beloved nation and people.

Back in Shabin Karahisar, Mgrditch's five children all found partners and got married. We believe that Mgrditch's wedding to Nazeli Ozanian preceded the marriages of his children. My grandmother, Anna, wed Sarkis Sergenian in 1890. In 1892, Anna and Sarkis became the parents of Victoria. Andon's birth followed in May of 1894, Aghavni in June 1896, Kaloust in June of 1899, my mother Ardemis in May of 1902, and finally Souren in 1904.

Meanwhile, Mgrditch began a second family with Nazeli. They had two daughters named Armenouhi (married name Kelerchian) and Mariam (married name unknown) and a son named Yervant. All of the children escaped the Genocide of 1915 and the girls eventually landed in France. Yervant was married in Tbilisi Georgia, to an Armenian girl from Erzurum with his famous uncle, Antranik, in attendance at the ceremony and celebration. Antranik hosted the reception.[3]

To conclude the story of Mgrditch and Nazeli Papazian, my mother's maternal grandfather and step-grandmother, I shall recount an embarrassing tale of family chicanery. In 1907, shortly after the untimely death of Anna's husband, Sarkis Sergenian (my grandfather) (by natural causes we are told), Anna was struggling to keep the household together. She had inherited the farm, land, house and savings. Meanwhile, at the Papazian household during that same time, Mgrditch's children with Nazeli were all teenagers. We are not certain if any of the youngsters had married. We know that during this period, Nazeli's brother, Antranik, participated in guerrilla campaigns against the Turks, and occasionally sought refuge in the safe haven of nearby Bulgaria.

Late in 1907, the tension and hostility intensified between the Turks and the patriots led by Antranik. Mgrditch and Nazeli planned to flee Shabin Karahisar and abandon Turkey for the relative safety of Bulgaria. We are not sure if the Papazian children were included in these plans. Nazeli had some knowledge of her famous brother's victories against the Turks, and knew of his "hideouts" in Bulgaria. She and her family were in some danger because of her relationship with Antranik.

Mgrditch and Nazeli visited Anna before leaving. Upon their departure from Anna Sergenian's home, Anna discovered that the "family fortune" (probably cash, gold, and jewelry) which was likely hidden or buried, had suddenly disappeared. After Anna uncovered her father's misdeed, she informed the local police who called the police in Constantinople. Remarkably, Mgrditch was found and detained, and the treasure recovered. It was not known how much of the family fortune was returned to Anna.

Mgrditch and Nazeli continued on to Bulgaria and settled outside of Varna. My mother Ardemis was unsure why her grandfather had attempted such an unsavory act. Perhaps a portion of the savings was his own, or from Nazeli's dowry. Unfortunately, we will never know the full and true story behind Mgrditch and Nazeli's seemingly scandalous action.

My great-grandfather Mgrditch and his second wife Nazeli lived out their lives in peace in a small home in Varna. The couple was spared the horrors of the genocide in 1915, but was kept informed. General Antranik visited them regularly when he sought sanctuary in the Balkans.[4]

Neighbors in Varna described Nazeli as a "strong-willed woman with raucous ways."[5] Mgrditch was depicted as a dark-skinned, silver-haired man of average stature and a mild disposition; a perfect complement to his fiery wife. Nazeli died just a few months before her great brother's death.[6] Antranik's last words were uttered on August 31, 1927, when he declared his desire to be buried in the hills or mountains of his beloved Armenia.[7] If this was not possible, his final wish was that his gravesite be next to his sister Nazeli.[8] Neither initially occurred, as Antranik's second wife, Nevart Kurkjian, whom he had married on March 15, 1922 in Paris France, had his remains enclosed in an oaken coffin to be taken to Armenia. The government in Moscow, however, prevented the transfer. Nevart then had the remains taken from the United States by ship to France and buried in Pere Lachaise Cemetery in Paris. Above his grave stood an imposing statue carved in marble of the great general mounted atop his stallion.[9]

After Antranik's death in 1927, Nevart returned to her native Bulgaria. In the spring of 2000, Antranik's remains were exhumed and taken to the Independent Republic of Armenia for internment. The brave hero of the Armenian Genocide was at last to rest in his homeland. As we commemorated the 1700th anniversary of Christianity in Armenia, General Antranik, who would be remembered as the fearless and fabled patriot who dedicated his life as a beacon of hope to all Armenians, would have his final wish fulfilled.[10]

As for Mgrditch, we have no knowledge of his last days or death. It is probable that he died in Varna and is buried alongside his wife. His descendants have not had the opportunity to seek out and visit his grave. Hopefully one day, one of us, his heirs, will do so. For he is the only one of my direct ancestors other than my mother and father who has a gravesite. It would give me deep personal satisfaction to kneel, pray and pay homage to him and all of my kin. The remains of all the others have been strewn with the winds into time immemorial.

Chapter 3

Efkere: Avedis' Homeland

Although my father lived only 20 years or so in Efkere, he was in spirit rooted firmly to his native soil and to its people and culture for the rest of his life. He would forever remain a proud Efkeretsi.

Efkere is situated on the fringe of the fabled cave region of Cappadocia. The earliest Christian dwellings and churches, which lay burrowed in the conical mounds and hills, may still be explored throughout this area. Today they are a popular tourist destination. The dwellings and churches situated in the caves date back at least to the second and third centuries.

Efkere, at the time of my father's birth in 1890, was a picturesque, small village with a population of about two or three thousand. According to a late 1800 Ottoman census, the hamlet was divided into

11

five distinct neighborhoods. Four of these districts housed the 500 Armenian families in Efkere. The fifth was inhabited by the 50 Turkish families who had for many years cohabitated with their Armenian countrymen.

The Armenian village was perched on a multi-terraced hillside at an elevation of about 500 feet. The city, then and now, is split into a west and east side by a brook which traversed the center of town. This stream is called Darsiak Suyu and as it meanders in its north to south direction, it passes below Soorp Stepanos Church, and is interrupted by two water mills. Some of the flow of the river is diverted upstream (to the northwest) and forms a small lake called Haft, or in Turkish, Efkere Goleti.

The stream and lake together provide the means to irrigate the land of Efkere. The village scene is an attractive study in contrast. Stone dominates all the buildings and streets but its harshness is softened by the lush vegetation and ample groves of forests. An open area adjacent to Lake Haft was a popular gathering place for the Armenian villagers in Efkere prior to the Genocide of 1915. Here the townspeople would celebrate festivals or feast days such as Easter with music and dance- hence the name – Bar Galler – the Dance Gallery.

Most of the homes in Efkere look alike, for they were built with the same stone blocks, and they are of the same general design. The streets and pathways of the village were hilly and narrow. Walls of stone lined many of the streets giving the homes behind them a guarded appearance.

Even the pavements of the streets and of the steps which provide access to the various levels of the hilly town make use of the same tan-white stone blocks. Efkere had, and still evokes, a formidable fort-like look of strength which surprisingly blends pleasantly with its softer pastoral landscape. In the spring, shades of green and yellow meld hillside to hillside. The sparkling azure of the lakes and the brilliant Anatolian sky add a finishing peaceful touch to the secluded village. Efkere was a haven to its 500 Armenian families and they believed that within its borders, they were sheltered from harm.

For many centuries in Efkere, the Muslim Ottoman families co-existed with their Christian Armenian neighbors in relative peace. Just a two-minute walk from Soorp Stepanos in East Efkere stood a very old Mosque. I understand that only its ruins remain today. Efkere was a village seeped strongly in its Armenian heritage, but this was still Turkey and by the turn of the 20th century, Efkere was surrounded by Turkish villages and towns, and was engulfed by the Turkish language and culture. Almost like an island, Efkere stood proudly and defiantly aloof from its Islamic rules and spoke its own dialect of Armenian within the confines of its' protective walls. The Armenians always sustained themselves as Armenians in Efkere. Efkere, along with Munjusun and a handful of other Armenian villages in Kayseri (Gesarya), was able to maintain its Armenian Christian religion, culture, traditions and tongue. The Efkeretsis successfully resisted all efforts to be absorbed into the yoke of their governing subjugators.

Gesarya in general and Efkere in particular, were renowned for the high quality of their Armenian educational facilities. Beside the religious learning centers of Soorp Stepanos and the Vank (Seminary) of Soorp Garabed, both boy and girl schools existed and thrived for many decades in Efkere. Among others, Nahabed Rousinian, the brilliant Armenian intellectual of the 19th century was born and schooled in Efkere, before continuing his higher education in Paris. Later, Rousinian's prolific pen set forth the stirring words exalting the sacred soil and site of the Catholicate of Cilicia. The poem so inspired composer G. Yeranian that he wrote the music to Rousinian's text, and the result is the anthem Armenians still sing with ardent fervor, "Giligia."

A. <u>Soorp Garabed Vank</u>

The founding of Efkere is believed to have its roots during the conquests of Alexander the Great around 330 BC. However, the word "Efkere", Greek in lineage- "Yevkaria" – (which translates into "sacred" or "sanctuary"), also appears to indicate the spiritual significance of the site. It is believed that St. Thaddeus, one of Christ's Apostles, brought the relic

14

bones of John the Baptist to a hillside cave (which later became the Soorp Garabed Vank (Monastery)) for safekeeping in the middle of the first century.

Later, during the last years of the third century, Efkere and Soorp Garabed Vank witnessed the birth of Armenian Christian enlightenment and national unity under the guidance of Saint Gregory the Illuminator. St. Gregory had converted the pagan Armenian King Dertad to Christianity. The King and his army traveled across Armenia to Gesarya with Gregory. There, at a conclave of Christian bishops, St. Gregory was first ordained as a bishop, and then elected "Hayrabed", which translates to "head father" or chief bishop. Later the title of "Catholicos" was adopted to signify the position as head of the Armenian Church.

St. Gregory was the ninth "Hayrabed in line" to be elected as the church's highest bishop since the death of Thaddeus the Apostle late in the First Century. After his election, St. Gregory set out on missionary endeavors. It is said that he began his passage back to the land of Ararat in Efkere. At the same site where the Apostle Thaddeus preached, Gregory placed a cross and founded the Soorp Garabed Vank (named for the "Forerunner.") Later in his travels he found another place of sanctuary for the relic bones of John the Baptist in Mush, an Armenian city in Turkey. In Mush, he founded another Soorp Garabed Vank at the site of a pagan temple. Both Vanks (seminaries) in Efkere and Mush were, and still are, considered sacred locations for Armenians, second only to Etchmiadzin.

Professor Robert Hewsen, the noted scholar of Armenian geography and history, describes Soorp Garabed in Efkere as, "at one time, the wealthiest, most frequented by pilgrims and most sacred shrine outside of Etchmiadzin." Today, Soorp Garabed lies in desolation and ruins beyond barbed wire and within the confines of a Turkish military post.

B. Soorp Stepanos Church

Religious manuscripts indicate that throughout time, Efkere had many churches and chapels in addition to its main church, Soorp Stepanos. Two smaller churches, Soorp Sarkis and Soorp Kevork, were mentioned in religious writings dating back to 1683. These were churches fashioned or carved from within the Cappodocian caves, which dotted the landscape. Remnants of these churches, which were located near Soorp Stepanos, still exist today.

A Catholic church, the Uniate Armenian Church of Efkere, also existed at one point prior to 1915. Records indicate that Zeki Ghalfyi, a resident of the neighboring village of Munjusun, constructed this Roman Catholic chapel. Pre-1915 Efkere also had three other churches, Soorp Theodore, Soorp Mercherios and Soorp Eliza (an open-air chapel) that were used on particular feast days.

As for Soorp Stepanos, records indicate that it was first built in 1683. It was destroyed and rebuilt at least twice. In 1831, a severe earthquake almost completely demolished Soorp Stepanos. It is unclear if it was rebuilt on its original site. The present building was constructed in 1871. The cornerstone in the northwest corner of the church is partially buried beneath the foundation – and its inscriptions are difficult to read. However, the marker appears to be much older than the present buildings. The church was built using the same whitish-gray stones used in building the village's homes. The stone blocks have been fashioned into cubic shapes and are approximately 15" x 30" x 15" in height, width and depth. The church was shaped in the traditional cruciform (free standing cross) design and topped by a dome.

The church's dome has collapsed (since at least 1919) and the main door, which is a recent construction of unadorned wooden planks) remains locked. Stone and brick blocks seal the street level windows. Presently, a Turk privately owns the grounds and building. Apparently he tries to be accommodating and when available will permit entrance to the church.

During my journey to Historic Armenia in June of 1998, the blocked windows and doors prevented me from seeing the interior of Soorp Stepanos. With great sadness I was only able to peer through the glassless windows on the church's second level from the roof of an adjoining building. I could distinguish two beautiful oval frescos, below the crest of the fallen dome. The church stands at the peak of one of Efkere's hills. It is east of the stream Darsiak Suyu and overlooks Western Efkere.

The dimensions of the church are roughly as follows: It stands some 40 feet high (without the dome) and it is approximately 110 feet long and 60 feet wide. The bell tower, parish house, adjoining schools, crosses; khatchkars and any other religious symbols on the exterior have been demolished and removed. Considerable stone rubble remains on the cleared area to the right side (north) of the church. A private home stands to its immediate left. This home may be remnants of the parish house and bell tower.

In Armen Aroyan's videotape entitled "Legendary Armenian Towns," Efkere and various scenes of the interior Soorp Stepanos are shown. The floor of the church is strewn with earth, and overgrown with vegetation. A tree towers skyward to some 30 feet. The altar is no longer discernible. However, the walls, windows and doorframes are profusely adorned with beautiful ornamental stone carvings. The interior walls glow with its original light pink texture.

Soorp Stepanos is the church where my father was baptized, served as an altar boy, was married to Vartouhi, and where their daughter, Mariam, was baptized. This was the church of the Sarajians.

C. The City of Efkere

Today, Efkere's natural beauty resembles what it must have looked like before the Armenians were forced to leave. It is still a pretty rural hamlet. However the spirit, energy, art, music and culture of the Armenians have been silenced. What is worse is that the local Kurds and Turks abuse and exploit what our ancestors were made to leave behind. The Turkish and Kurdish buildings are constructed from blocks and stones stolen from Armenian churches. Holy grave markers, still bearing the carved ornamental design of the Armenian cross, are used as pathways and doorway steps.

The Armenians of Efkere were skilled craftsmen, merchants and farmers. The blacksmiths forged the iron skeleton that laced the stones of Soorp Stepanos in an invisible wall of strength. The women in the village were expert rug weavers. Efkere was also renowned for its skill and industry in the pigeon trade. Thousands of pigeons darkened the skies of Efkere at the turn of the 20th century. Today those famous stone pigeon coops of Efkere which still dot the hills stand as muted sentinels void of the flocks they sheltered. There are no Armenian Efkeretsis to nurture and harvest the birds. The unique stone-block coops with their unusual stepped and angled roof-perches today provide shelter for only a few wild birds. The birds and their crumbling shelters serve as a cruel and harsh reminder of what was once, and will never be again.

On the higher slopes of Efkere the town's residents once gloried in the majestic sight of Mt. Arkeos. The mountains' snow capped peaks soar abruptly skyward to better than 13,000 feet. In all of Turkey only the two peaks of the Ararats stand taller. In fact, Mt. Arkeos is often referred to as the little Ararat of Gesarya. The glaciers on the peaks provide the entire area with its' primary source of water.

Presently the inhabitants of Efkere are a mix of Kurds and Turks. As in most Armenian villages following the massacres and deportations of the Genocide, the Ottomans "imported" Kurdish tribes from eastern Anatolia. In this manner the Turkish government dispersed the "dangerous ethnic Kurdish tribe's people" of the east, and re-populated the ghost towns which had been evacuated by the purged Armenians.

When questioned today, these Turks and Kurds profess little knowledge concerning the fate of the Armenians in 1915. They answer innocently "yes-these were Armenian towns but they (the Armenians) went away". "We heard they were good people and wish they were still here." The Kurds and Turks live today on a day-to-day, hand to mouth life style. They use, re-use and abuse the land and structures. They seldom endeavor to improve, or create either by labor or culture, the beloved soil of our forefathers.

Perhaps it is, as it should be. Only God knows what mournful spirits still haunt the blood stained earth of beautiful Efkere.

Chapter 4

The Sarajians and their Life in Efkere: 1890-1913

Little is known about young Avedis and his family at the close of the 19th century. Although the Armenians were certainly a subjugated people in Turkey, we have no knowledge about how the Sarajians suffered from the wide-spread periodic massacres of the "Red Sultan," Abdul Hamid.

As mentioned earlier, the populace of Efkere was mostly Armenian. Outside the village, the language and script was always Turkish. It was said that you would be subject to arrest if you spoke the Armenian language in the city of Gessarya. Within the confines of the village of Efkere, a good deal of freedom seemed to abound, but it was always tempered with caution. The townspeople spoke in their particular dialect of Armenian, which was freely intermixed with Turkish jargon and slang.

We are fairly certain that young Avedis finished his primary education in Efkere. We know that the Soorp Stepanos Church had a school, called the "Torkomian-Akbarian School" which was built in 1880. In 1901, existing school records indicate that 170 students attended the school. One of these students may have been a youth of 10 years of age, Avedis Sarajian.

Besides his schooling, Avedis, along with his older brother Minas, was required to help his father in his labors. Avedis' father, Dikran Sarajian, was in the "dry goods" business. He sold cloth, dyes, threads, buttons, shoes as well as some "finished, or ready to wear clothing." It is believed that Dikran toiled at his trade from house to house, rather than from a store. It is also believed that he traveled from village to village, for sales and bartering.

Later on in his life, Avedis would recall to his wife Ardemis that his father, although loving and protective, was paternally stern and strict towards him. But in typical parental balance, Avedis' mother, Marian, was patient and forgiving toward her spirited baby. Although strong-willed, and sometimes even stubborn, Avedis was always respectful. He was also a strongly religious child, attending church faithfully and serving as an altar boy at Soorp Stepanos. His ties to his church and to his God would guide him for the rest of his life.

When Avedis left Efkere for America, his mother gave him a pocket-sized Bible printed with the tiniest Armenian type. It remained with him, and served to comfort him all his years in America. Avedis deeply cherished the Book, for both what it was, and from where and whom it came. When Avedis died in 1967, Ardemis placed that Bible in his hand. He was buried holding the final physical vestige of his birth land, his family, and his faith.

In the early 1900's, conscription into the Turkish army was mandatory unless the draftee was able to buy out his term of service. Avedis entered the military in about 1909 or 1910. The normal period of service was two years. Ethnic or "gavoor" soldiers, which was a demeaning Turkish description of Armenians, Kurds, Greeks and other minorities, were forbidden to carry arms. Instead, they were assigned the most menial tasks of army life. They dug ditches, cleaned latrines, carried equipment and struggled to keep out of the way of the regular Turkish troops. Their status was akin to cattle, or beasts of burden, and they were treated as such. For a non-Turk to endure his two years of service, and return home unscathed, was unusual.

Avedis served in this degrading capacity, and was stationed in military frontiers as far away as Albania. After he completed his required term, Avedis returned home and rejoined his father and brother in their family business. About a year later, sometime in 1912, when he was 21 years old, Avedis courted and then married his first wife Vartouhi. We believe she was a local girl.

Shortly after Avedis and Vartouhi were wed, the world political situation worsened. World War I was on the horizon, and even the remote villages within Turkey began feeling the impact. With the Turks already entwined in the Balkan intrigues, and the young Turks plotting their pan-Islamic schemes, it became apparent that increased conscription and re-conscription would soon occur. Sketchy details and rumors of Armenian youths being sacrificed for the sake of the war effort frightened every Armenian family. Would their conscripted young men ever return? The Turks had found still another way to answer their "Armenian Question."

After a family conference, Dikran and Mariam Sarajian made a monumental decision regarding Avedis. It would change his life forever. Since Avedis was expected to be recalled into the army, they decided to send him to America. Unknown to Avedis (and to the rest of the family), Vartouhi has just become pregnant. Immediate plans were put into effect. Avedis was given enough money to journey from Gesarya to Ankara and on to Constantinople. There he would seek out his uncle, his mother's brother, who had a successful business in Constantinople. The uncle, together with his wife and two sons, would help Avedis procure the necessary funds and papers to make the crossing to America. Once, there, Avedis would find his mother's second brother Jevan, who had immigrated earlier, and now resided in New York City. The plan was that Avedis would work with all diligence to accumulate the funds necessary to help bring the whole family to America and freedom.

We do not know if Avedis was fully compliant with the plan, but knowing his nature, his strong will and stubborn determination, I feel certain that he would not have undertaken such a responsibility without being in full accord of its' design. It certainly was a wild dream, but it had been done successfully before. America!

Sometime in 1913 Avedis left his wife, family, friends and Efkere forever. This chapter in his youth now closed, and the heartbreak and joys of a new life awaited him in America.

Chapter 5

Ardemis in Shabin Karahisar

A. Sarkis, Anna and Their Children

S arkis Sergenian and Anna Papazian were wed sometime around 1890 or 1891. They set up their home in Shabin Karahisar. Sarkis was about 23 years old, Anna about 18 or 19. Sarkis had inherited some fertile land on which he grew wheat, raised the usual domestic animals and tended his fruit orchards. The family grew and prospered.

Anna and Sarkis' first child, a girl, whom they named Victoria, was born in 1892. Every two or three years hence, Anna bore another baby. Andon was born in 1894, Aghavni (Khosrofitooght) in 1896, Kaloust in 1899, Ardemis is 1902 and finally Souren in 1904. Within a twelve-year span, Anna and Sarkis had six healthy children. While all the children survived, Sarkis, barely 40 years old, died tragically of natural causes in 1907. Victoria the eldest was 15 and Souren, the baby, was only 3 when their father died. Shortly thereafter, Anna either abandoned or leased the farm in Shabin Karahisar and returned to her birthplace Tokat, with all six children. She felt more comfortable with her friends and relatives in Tokat. Anna did, however, travel frequently to Shabin Karahisar. The youngest of the children spent much of their formative years in their mother's city of Tokat. In 1909, Victoria, now 17 or 18, married in Shabin Karahisar to a Mr. Dugerian. In time, she gave birth to a son, Kevork, and then to a daughter, Seranoush. Her union was, unfortunately, an unhappy one.

Back in Tokat, Andon, the elder son, was getting his basic education in the highly respected Jesuit school, and he also found a job at a local factory making shoes. Aghavni contributed to the family by creating and selling elegant embroidery pieces. Kaloust, the bright, young scholar of the family had also been admitted to the Jesuit school of Tokat. Ardemis, now about six or seven, and baby brother Souren, (about four or five), did their part by shelling walnuts at the local nut house of Tokat. The two youngest Sergenians worked there until one day the Turkish boss caught Souren eating some of the walnuts rather than shelling them, and angrily fired both children. Ardemis was using her salary to help pay for her schooling. As a result, she did not achieve much more than a few years of formal education.

Sometime in 1911, Anna returned to Shabin Karahisar with the purpose of selling the farm. Andon, Ardemis and Souren made the trip with their mother. At the courthouse, Turkish officials told her that she could not sell any property until her youngest child became 18 years old. Souren was now seven or eight. Anna planned her return to Tokat. She left Ardemis with her older sister, Hripsimeh Odabashian and her family, in Karahisar. It is unclear why. Anna and Souren traveled back to Tokat. Upon her return Anna found that her middle daughter, Aghavni, had married. We have no record of the boy's name. Aghavni was about 17 years old.

Andon, now almost 18, had made up his mind to journey to America. Perhaps the threat of having to enter Turkish military service helped him to decide. There is some discrepancy about Andon's whereabouts during the next few years. Some believe he came to America, left and then later re-entered the United States. It is fairly certain that Andon eventually (in 1915-1916) joined the American-Armenian division of the French Foreign Legion volunteers, and fought against the German and Turkish forces. Andon fought along with General Antranik's army in Anatolia.

About the same time, Victoria, the eldest, returned to Tokat from Karahisar with her two children Kevork and Seranoush. Victoria had left her husband, Mr. Dugerian, who had a terrible reputation. He was a heavy drinker, a gambler, and would often abuse his wife and children. After returning to Tokat, Victoria became seriously ill. She had contracted cholera. Anna nursed her daughter and cared for her two grandchildren. Victoria recovered, but sadly Anna became afflicted with the same illness, and died in 1912. She was barely 40 years old; about the same age her husband had been when he died some five years previously.

The Sergenians were orphans. After her recovery, Victoria, now twenty years old, took control of the household. She urged Kaloust to help enroll Souren in the Jesuit school. Andon was probably in Philadelphia at this point.

Aghavni was married and living nearby in Tokat. She was just seventeen years old. Ardemis, now ten years old, was living with Aunt Hripsimeh in Karahisar. However, a few years later in February of 1915, her family arranged her marriage to Hampartsum Balian who was seventeen or eighteen years old. The Balians were friends of the Sergenians and the families hoped that Hampartsum could avoid service in the Turkish military if he were married.

The conditions of this union had Ardemis, not yet thirteen, move into the Balian family home in Tamzara. There, Ardemis was put under the protective custody of mother Balian. Ardemis even slept with her mother-in-law. The marriage was not to be consummated until it was determined that young Hampartsum would not have to serve in the military. As it turned out, this was not possible and Hampartsum was conscripted into the Turkish army. He never returned. Ardemis remained in Tamzara with the Balian family until June 1915.

Chapter 6

Shabin Karahisar: Up Close and Personal

The history of Shabin Karahisar dates back before the birth of Christ. The Romans, during their forays into the Near East passed through northern (Lesser) Armenia. As they conquered and advanced, they built ramparts and fortresses to secure strategic positions. When the legions of Caesar overran Shabin Karahisar they built a bastion atop the mountainous outcropping that became known as the "Pert" or the Fort.[11]

At this time, Lesser Armenia was ruled by a Roman appointed king. The king was from a wealthy Jewish family, and his wife was the infamous Salome. We can say, therefore, without any great pride, that the seductress Salome, was at least for a time, the queen of the Armenians.

Shabin Karahisar is located in north central Anatolia. The city is located high in the Pontus Mountains, its elevation exceeding 5,800 feet. The Pontus Mountains are an impressive range, boasting peaks better than two miles high. The mountains stretch in a convoluted, meandering manner from west to east across the northern ridge of the Anatolian fault for more than a thousand miles. Their northern slopes face the expanse of the Black Sea.

Shabin Karahisar's current population totals almost 25,000. It lies 63 miles directly south of Giresun on the Black Sea. It is situated 26 miles north of the main highway between Erzinga (75 miles to the east) and Sepastia or Sivas (125 miles to the west). There are a number of small villyets surrounding Karahisar. The most famous is Tamzara, which is well-known among Armenians for the famous dance that bears its name. Tamzara is just two miles to the north of Karahisar. My maternal grandmother's place of birth, the city of Tokat, lies about 125 miles west of Karahisar, just north of Sepastia.

Shabin Karahisar lies within the governing province of Sepastia (Sivas). In June of 1998, my wife, Mary, and I, together with my wife's sister Berjouhi, her husband Krikor, our Prelate Archbishop Mesrop Ashjian, and some close friends, were fortunate to spend several hours in Shabin Karahisar. This nostalgic and emotion-filled visit occurred during our Pilgrimage to Historic Armenia, led by Armen Aroyan.

When we visited, we had already explored Historic Armenia for two weeks. We had concluded our easterly wanderings, had headed north through Ani and Kars, and now, we were on our westerly journey back toward Istanbul via the northern route. The course directed us through Erzurum and Erzinga, then diverted northward to Shabin Karahisar. After our late afternoon visit in the Karahisar area we eventually back-tracked to the highway and continued finally to Sepastia. The bus ride through the mountains of Erzinga and adjacent to Mount Sebouh, afforded us a vista of unbelievable scenic splendor. The wildness of the northern mountains, the ravines, and gorges, together with the rush of the untamed Euphrates and its tributaries was breathtaking.

This Anatolia was unlike the gentile slopes of the tranquil hills of southern Anatolia, and the placid plains, which marked the gateway to the deserts of Iraq and Iran. Our highway travel took us westward from the attractively rebuilt city of Erzinga (rebuilt due to the devastating earthquake in 1939) toward the ancient Armenian city of Sepastia. Just short of the halfway point of this major east-west artery, we turned north and delved deeper into the Pontus Mountains, heading towards the vast waters of the Black Sea, some 100 miles away. Fortunately, our concerns about the local back roads to Shabin

Karahisar being impassable in some areas proved unfounded. However, the steep climbs and diving dips through the myriad of gorges were tortuous, and the bus labored in its serpentine twisting trek to Karahisar.

We passed through no villages, towns, or even isolated homesteads in our one hour, 26-mile passage through these highlands. The road surface changed from macadam to gravel, and then to compacted soil. Many of the sharp, sweeping turns were void of guardrails and a driver's miscalculation could easily result in disaster. Our information regarding this road was that winter motoring was "not advised."

Because these mountains seemed devoid of habitation, I was startled to see an impressive new dam and hydroelectric plant. Earlier on, while still on the Erzinga to Sivas highway, we had passed along and eventually over an emerald green river. I thought it was the Euphrates, but was then informed that it was the Wolf River, a tributary of the great "Yeprat." The Wolf starts as a small insignificant stream in the northernmost high country of the Pontus Mountains near the Black Sea. The stream spurts southward increasing in velocity, cascading and cutting deep rocky gorges near Karahisar. Its torrential flow swells as it continues its southerly journey for more than 25 miles. Here the Wolf eases into a long and peaceful lake, confined by the steel and concrete abutment, which looms ahead. The river, now tamed and tranquil due to the hydroelectric plant, re-emerges beyond the dam. It will continue merging with other streams until it blends into the mighty Euphrates.

As we continued our journey to Karahisar, we passed along stockpiles of sewer or water pipes. This unexpected evidence of encroaching civilization tempered the spell of unspoiled nature. However, we did not see any workmen or heavy machinery nearby. Nor did we see homes or habitation of any kind.

Motoring onward, further north, the landscape gradually transformed from beautiful to simply spectacular. Our bus snaked up and down, from mountaintop to valley plain. The vistas passed before us in a magical panorama. The hues contrasted rather than blended. The craggy slopes and cliffside slopes bore the earthy red and rusty coloration only exhibited by mineral rich soil. The forests were primed in their springtime verdant green. Clusters of conifers, evergreens and poplars crowded into tight orchards separated from each other by magenta tinted stony outcroppings. Each element stood out, defined and precise, three dimensional as only nature can ascribe. To add further drama to the scene, acres of wheat fields abounded, not only on level hilltops or in valleys, but also along severely sloped mountainsides. The shimmering reflections of the wheat's golden grains highlighted the neighboring greens and reds with a wash of luminescence. Everything sparkled. Even the air crackled with sweet purity.

I have experienced in my own lifetime, (as have most people, I suppose), visual-emotional "auras," where all things about me take on a special appearance. These "auras" are always preceded by a heightened state of all of my natural senses. My ability to see, hear, smell, feel and even discern is acutely sharpened; all sensation and images are burned into my memories as a permanent, indelible record of a special time. Most likely, these feelings, which overcame me during this time in Shabin Karahisar, were influenced by my excited and sensitized frame of mind. I had just viewed and absorbed the beautiful land of my forefathers and then, somehow, I recompose these impressions into my own personal depiction of our ancestral paradise.

Actually, this "aura" must have been the result of an accumulation of sensitivities. Never before had I experienced such a continuing flood of emotion within a limited time span. It was as if feelings had become stronger than thought, and my body in touch with the soul. I was overcome as we drove to Shabin Karahisar. This feeling had already overtaken me during Badarak (Holy Mass) in Soorp Gregory Church in Gesarya, while standing alongside my father's church, Soorp Stepanos in Efkere, atop the mountain monastery of Soorp Garabed in Mush, while visiting Soorp Avak in Erzinga, viewing the ruins of Ani, and when paying homage to the Biblical Mountain of Noah, Mt. Ararat. Celebrating requiem mass at the majestic Holy Cross Church on the isle of

Aghtamar in the azure waters of Lake Van was also a life-changing experience for me.

I can rationalize these sensations and sensibilities clinically as "externally stimulated cerebral highs." But rather than this scientific conclusion, I have resolved to treasure and cherish these "super" feelings in a far different way. I will forever I remember them as my own personal glimpses into Eden. How fortunate we all were. How fortunate I was, to have been a part of it.

Continuing on, most of the mountains we saw unfolded in a contiguous range of peaks and valleys. Occasionally a single solitary mass of stone would spurt dramatically skyward. Standing tall, steeply inclined, definitely alone, as if a sentinel, its mission forever to guard the land about it. In the distance stood one such singular mountain. Atop its crest remain the ruins of the Fortress, the "pert" of Karahisar.

Still some two miles south of Karahisar we stopped to glory at the sight of a waterfall to our west. We stood on the roadside peering down a deepening valley to a waterfall pulsating out from a crevice high in an amphitheater of granite, and then plunging hundreds feet to a basin below. The water did not overflow its surrounding semi circular wall of stone. Rather, it erupted forth, powerful as a shooting siphon. I guess the waterfall was an appropriate signpost as we approached Karahisar.

As we drove through the outskirts of Shabin Karahisar we passed buildings and homes unlike those in the rest of Anatolia. The structures here were made mostly of wood, topped with metal roofs - few were constructed of stone. Granite block homes had been the rule in most of Anatolia. Wood prevailed as the type of construction in Lesser Armenia. We got a fleeting glimpse of the "University of Shabin Karahisar" on a hilltop to our east. The school appeared as a grouping of newly built attractive brick buildings, just a bit south of the city limits. Archbishop Mesrop, once again, had the research knowledge to point out the university. I was exhilarated as we entered the village of my maternal ancestors. The signposts indicated that Shabin Karahisar now boasted a population of 23,400. I would guess that today's inhabitants are in large measure Turks, with a smattering of Kurds and a few others. In 1915 the population was estimated to be 15,000. Of these, 7000 were Turks, 7000 Armenians, and the remaining mostly Greeks and a few Jews.

I have read other journals that put the estimate at 12,000 Turks, 6000 Armenians and 3000 Greeks. The Armenians always occupied the slopes and craggy nooks on the side of the mountain. Hence, their homes faced the favorable southerly winds, an important factor in mountain construction. The village in 1915 was divided into "wards." The Armenians lived on the hillside wards, which bordered the trail that led to the top of the mountain and the fort. The Turks owned the flatlands directly to the west. The primary route northward, toward Giresun, was "Main Street," as it passed through the city. Actually, the Armenians, to their advantage, looked down upon the Turks. Most importantly, their access to the fort atop the Mountain was direct and unimpeded.

Shortly after entering the city, I was able to enjoy my first view of the mountains and the "Pert." The bus stopped, and we disembarked. We all took videos and pictures and I collected soil and rocks to bring back home to share with my family and other Shabin Karahisaritzes.

Archbishop Mesrop Ashjian offered a memorial mass, perhaps the first ever said here in Shabin Karahisar since the savagery of June 1915. The Archbishop collected wild flowers and placed them on a flat- topped boulder, then he lit a candle and burned incense on this makeshift but natural open-air alter.

With the power of the "Pert" rising above us, we could not help but recall, if only for a few fleeting moments, the stories and tales of sacrifice that were forever sealed along the slopes of Karahisar's fabled mountain. We prayed. The mass was offered for all the martyrs that perished in 1915. It was then offered for the family of Nubar Zoryan, my fellow Karahisartsi, and my fellow pilgrim on this journey. Remembered also were Aram Haigaz, the great participant and recorder of the Armenians' attempt to defend themselves against the Turks during a battle at the Pert, and the never to be forgotten hero, legend and indomitable freedom fighter, General Antranik Ozanian. And finally, we memorialized my family, those that died here, and those who lived but never forgot.

Krikor and Berjouhi Pidedjian sang the requiem to the dead, the "Hoki- Hankist" with beautiful, soulful measure as they assisted the Archbishop in his prayers. We cried. We embraced each other, and carefully memorialized these precious moments so we could call them back at a later time, and share them with those who would understand. This experience weakened me; it was overwhelming. I thanked my spiritual shepherd, the Archbishop, and my brother-in-law and sister-in law for their part in this solemn service. Archbishop Mesrop distributed the altar wildflowers to Baron Nubar and to me. I thanked and kissed Armen Aroyan, that wonderful man, whose intense love and compassion of our land, Historic Armenia, and its' people, made my pilgrimage possible.

Most of all, I thanked God for permitting me to walk this land, to see its' beauty, smell its' fragrance and even hear its' "whispers." I promised Him I would never forget it. And I thanked Him again for hearing our prayers for the peaceful repose of all our heroes. After the Hoki-Hankist was concluded we boarded the bus and continued on.

It soon became apparent that because of time constraints we would not be able to visit the hallowed ground of the "Pert." We could not even wander on foot through the Armenian or "Hye" section of Karahisar. I was already sad. Now a deepening depression engulfed me. Here I crossed ten thousand miles, and it took me almost sixty-eight years (my age), and "we did not have enough time." I consoled myself with the fact that a climb to the fort, even if permitted by the local police or militia, would be extremely arduous, and certainly time consuming. As far as walking the streets of our ancestors, well, we know all our homes were torched to the ground and churches disassembled and destroyed in 1915. The Turks had built their homes and mosques atop our firmaments, and over our dead. Another Turkish desecration, another attempt to erase the Armenians, and another Turkish attempt to hide their horrific crimes.

We drove through the "business section" of Karahisar, which became the town's main street. The sidewalks were broad, and paved in concrete. Trees were planted curbside and vehicles, mostly farm trucks and tractors, were parked bumper to bumper. The central area, although crowded, still gave the appearance of openness. The Anatolian sky and jagged peaks of the Pontus Mountains dominated. I felt "country," not "city." The air was tingly fresh, and the skies sparkled in a magical brilliance. It was an alpine setting, truly the province of the eagles and their aerie so well captured in Aram Haigaz's book, The Fall of the Aerie, about the Battle on the Pert.

Among the first buildings we passed was an apartment house or so it seemed. It was hard to imagine apartment houses in Karahisar. Shops of all sorts exhibited their wares neatly in storefronts. The citizens bustled about on foot, rushing here and there. This alone was conspicuously different from the towns we had visited in the south. Here we saw energy and it contrasted with the leisurely pace of lower Anatolia. Few women could be seen walking the streets. Apparently, Turkish village women remain homebound. After a mile or so we approached the crossroads, the center of the city. Here we passed several crowed busses. There was a sign noting the hospital. My wife, Mary, who had hurt her ankle and leg, spotted that signpost. She did not know yet that her ankle and leg were broken in two places after a mishap in the hills of Erzinga. I don't believe she would have permitted Turkish medical aid in any case.

Here also, located at the town circle (central area), was the town fountain. In the old days these springs or fountains were all important. Obviously, no plumbing meant no water in the house. Most villages were developed and grew around a central potable water spring. These areas became socially important, as neighbors exchanged greetings and news while filling their water pots and jugs. The fountain of Shabin Karahisar was designed somewhat like a gazebo. Four pillars supported a decorative roof. Benches surrounded it and it stood on a stone and concrete foundation. A decorated iron tube emerged from the ground and its' plumbing consisted of four faucets, one in each corner. The water flow was regulated by a bronze, squeeze-type on and off control. A few Turks were sitting about the fountain as we passed by in our bus.

At a fork in the road, the bus followed the "left fork." The "right fork" narrower and containing much less vehicle traffic, appeared to divert directly to the base of the mountain. This must have been the road to the Armenian ward and homesteads. If we had followed it, we would find the trail to the Pert. Instead, we stayed on the "major" road, which, I believe, continued all the way north to Giresun.

About a quarter mile past the town center, there suddenly emerged on our left side and in close proximity another grouping of peaks and cliffs. While I was entranced with the mountain of Shabin Karahisar, I had lost my focus of the total landscape. We were truly in the highlands of Hayastan.

Further to the east, past rolling hills and valleys, you could see a solitary jagged outcropping soaring skyward. The "Pert and its mountain" hovered directly above us, over our right shoulder. The buildings of the fort and its adjoining stone ramparts were clearly visible. I recall commenting that the Pert instilled in me a somber, foreboding chill. Back-lit by the sun, it seemed to harbor a dramatic bleak and dismal atmosphere. In actuality, the Fortress stood out as the last remaining vestige of ancient strength and power. It was impressive. The forlorn look I had perceived was of my own making. I could not help but recall the massacre of June 1915, when the Pert was mutated to become the cemetery of the last of its native "Karahisaritzes'." More than 2000 years of culture were erased in one month of terror.

What remains today is an unforgotten symbol of the Shabin Karahisar of the Armenians. The "Pert" is the very essence of the city, its history and its people. We continued on.

Our next destination was Tamzara. This village, famous for its rhythmic dance, is barely two miles north of Shabin Karahisar. Our aim was to find Soorp Kevork church, the only remaining church in the area. Our bus driver, Jemal, had found and visited this church a few years ago, but on this trip he somehow took a wrong turn. I was becoming anxious as we searched with no success. I had a personal stake in locating this church; my mother had been married in Soorp Kevork church in February 1915 to her first husband.

My mother had lived in her in-laws home in Tamzara during the spring of 1915. It was from here that Ardemis and her sister Victoria, with Victoria's two children, began their death march. Emotions again began welling up inside of me. Was it to be another emotional "revisitation," - a walk in my mother's footsteps? Or was it just another fruitless search. Jemal questioned a Turk on the road as to the church's location. Sadly we were informed that new road construction had demolished the church. Another Turk remarked that it was a beautiful building with a large and glorious chandelier. Disappointment! Another sacred piece of Armenian history gone forever. For 83 years the Turks have destroyed and desecrated.

As we drove through the narrow pathways north of Shabin Karahisar I reviewed my own memories about the "secret marriage" of Hampartsum Balian and Ardemis Sergenian. Unable to find the church at Tamzara where my mother had wed Mr. Balian, the pilgrimage bus returned toward Karahisar. My brother-in-law Krikor softened the edge of my sadness and disappointment by some rousing renderings of revolutionary songs. He sang of the wonderful victories of Antranik, with his spirited patriotic gusto. It was a fitting re-entrance into Karahisar.

The bus paused at the "aghpuir," (fountain or spring), where Nubar Zoryan and I disembarked, washed our faces and hands, and tasted the water of our ancestors' land. I filled a plastic bottle with the cold spring water. It would be my only gift, along with some soil, stones, wildflowers and grains of wheat to my friends and family back home. It would also be devotional tokens of remembrance for many of us as we prayerfully placed these pebbles and drops of spring water upon the graves of our beloved departed survivors.

All in all, I spent just a few hours here in Karahisar. I so tried to fill the void in my mind and heart, with all the sacred sights of my roots. I ached for more; this was just not enough. But it was ending, and it was at least something.

As we departed, with the Pert fading from view, I thanked God for giving me this time here. I had treaded on our holy ancestral soil, which was consecrated in blood almost a century ago. I had felt Karahisar, I had seen the Pert, and smelled the sweetness of its wild flowers. I had tasted the biting cold of its spring waters and heard its wind, its' birds, and the rustle of its trees. I had touched its soil and held its rocks. I have felt Karahisar.

I will remember, and tell all those who long for our "yergeer," our homeland, but cannot go. I have so much more than I had before, and I will never forget. It was goodbye to Shabin Karahisar, and farewell to Historic Armenia, but a part of me will remain there forever.

Chapter 7

Avedis Sets Sail

A vedis sailed from Constantinople to Piraeus, Greece late in 1913. From Piraeus he boarded another ship to Ellis Island, New York City, America. Avedis' sole obligation and concern was now to work hard, become successful and earn enough money to help his family immigrate to the magic land. In New York, Avedis found his Uncle Jevan, and within weeks he re-acquainted himself with other refugees from Efkere.

For some unknown reason most Efkeretsis settled in Detroit, but a smaller number stayed in New York, and most of them lived in Brooklyn. Uncle Jevan reunited Avedis with his former parish priest, Der Hayr Sahagian. The Der Hayr had also "escaped" from Turkey and emigrated, with his wife and five children to America. The youngest boy of the family was Edward Sahagian. Edward either knew, or worked for an Armenian restaurateur in Manhattan. Edward introduced Avedis to the restaurant owner, and Avedis was hired as an assistant cook. Avedis along with his new job "adopted" a new first name. Here in America, he would now be known as John.

For some reason or other, we have no further reference to Uncle Jevan. It is sad that the families never maintained or renewed contact. Jevan Kaloostian was the closest living relative we had in America, and we have no clue as to what happened to him.

As for Avedis, he was on his way. He had an American first name, and his first job as an American.

Chapter 8

Joyful News for Avedis

Sometime in 1914, Avedis heard he had become a father. Vartouhi had given birth to a beautiful, healthy baby girl. The baby was named Mariam, after Avedis' mother and she was christened in Soorp Stepanos Church. The happiness and joy which engulfed Avedis motivated him to work all the harder. Whatever he could save was sent to his family in Efkere. He lived and dreamt of having his loved ones together with him in the United States. Avedis missed them. He wrote to Vartouhi and to his mother and father, asking for a photograph of his baby Mariam, along with the rest of the family. Remarkably, the family was able to comply. Late in 1914 Avedis received a professional black and white postcard size portrait. It included his father and mother, one of his nephews, (the son of his sister), his wife and infant daughter (now 6 months old). Avedis

49

was overjoyed. This would be his first and only view of his daughter. Later in life Avedis would have that little 4" x 6" postcard photo enlarged. Eventually he had the enlargement colorized as well. The framed portrait always hung in our living room. This was the picture that brought tears to my father's eyes.

Chapter 9

Avedis' Life in America: 1914

Toward the end of 1914 Avedis deeply yearned to see his family again. By this time World War I raged in Europe and travel to and from Turkey, which was allied with Germany, was impossible. Avedis was now determined to work even harder. He continued sending money to Efkere, but without any assurance that it reached its destination. In less than two years Avedis had become a partner in the restaurant. He was also a partner of a boarding house on East 27th Street in Manhattan. The residents of the hotel were mostly Armenian refugees, who paid "John" whatever they could afford. The building also housed a "Pool Parlor" (billiards), on the street level.

During his early days in America, Avedis associated, as did most Armenian newcomers, almost exclusively with other Armenians. His closest

51

cronies were his kinsmen, immigrants from his home village of Efkere. One of his closest friends was his priest and former pastor of Soorp Stepanos, Der Hayr Mesrop Sahagian. The priest had fled Efkere with his wife, the Yeretzgin (wife of the priest) and their four sons and one daughter. Another close friend was Hagop Nergizian, who later became his best man when my parents married and Godfather to Dick, Mary and me. Still others included the families of Hagop Kalajian, Mardiros Touvalian, Paroog Sinamian, Simon Keleshian, Hagop Stepanian, Dadoor Papazian, Astigaha Cherikjian, Garabed Avedisian, and another old gentleman I can only identify by his first name, Misigagha.

My father's closest living relatives were the Yerganians, cousins who lived in Watertown, Massachusetts and another cousin Asadoor Sarajian who also lived in Watertown, Massachusetts. Again, we have no further information regarding Jevan Kaloostian, his uncle and his mother's brother.

Avedis remained active in the church, and politically aligned with the Armenian Revolutionary Federation (the Dashnag Party). His primary motivation, however, remained his desire to contact his family and then do his utmost to extricate them from Turkey.

Chapter 10

Death, Devastation and Despair: The Genocide as Seen from the United States

Sometime after April 1915, Avedis Sarajian, along with thousands of other Armenian refugees, learned of the unimaginable, unspeakable devastation which annihilated the whole Armenian nation in Turkey.

As in most cases, as it was in his, it was not a single loss in a family, or even a group, but the savage death and destruction of everything and everyone he knew. He learned, and I'm not sure how, that his wife, daughter, mother, father, brother and sister, their spouses and children, all his relatives and friends in Efkere were now dead.

They did not just die. Most were tortured, starved, beaten and drowned. Many were bayoneted, burned, shot, stabbed and gutted. Those who survived village mutilations were subjected to forced death marches. During these death marches, "they were marched out in the heat of summer and not given food or drink. They either died along the way or were sent into the Syrian Desert to locations such as Der Zor, where those who survived the forced marches were killed."[12] Driven and beaten until senseless, women were raped and degraded. The young girls and children were ravaged and then sold into servitude and slavery. They were expelled from their homes, churches, villages, towns and cities and marched into oblivion.

The tattered survivors of this hell became the lost souls of the world. They had lost everything: their families, their land, their culture, their history, their nation. They grieved for the remainder of their lives.

It was the time of deepest, darkest despair for all Armenians. It was the cataclysmic event in Armenian history. Quotes from the headlines of the New York Times, and the London Times read as follows: "Wholesale massacres of Armenians by Turks", July 28, 1915, LT, "Appeal to Turkey by Ambassador Morgenthau to stop massacres," April 27, 1915, N.Y. Times. "Armenians sent to desert to perish, Turks accused of planned extermination of whole population", NY Times. "People of Karahisar massacred, L.T. August 18, 1915. "Armenian women put up at auction", N.Y. Times,

September 29, 1915. "Committee on atrocities confirms tales of Armenian horrors." NY Times, Sept. 27, 1915.

On and on they read. Photographs of ragged women and starving children filled the front pages of western newspapers. Avedis heard, saw, read and wept. He became a tortured soul, desperately seeking answers where no answers were to be found. His mind and body writhed with the unceasing pangs of loss and guilt. Why, who, where, when, why, why, why?!

Our family, Mom, Dick, Mary and I know little of our father's search for answers. We are not sure who told him of the brutal carnage of his beloved family, or the fate of all the villagers in his beloved homeland. He hoped against hope, prayed constantly, cried and waited for some bit of news. But after a time it became apparent that it was monstrous but true, all were gone, and all was finished. Avedis never again heard from any family member.

Little is known, or recounted about Avedis during the next five years. I have heard that he spoke rarely and cried often. After all, he had little to live for. During the following months and from time to time, Avedis was called upon to help minister to his former parish priest, Father Sahagian. The Der Hayr was battling his own legions of demons which had ravaged his flock in Efkere. Although he had succeeded in saving his own family, the good Der

Hayr was caught in a maelstrom of guilt and depression. He would contact Avedis (who himself was despondent), and designate a rendezvous. They would meet at one or two o'clock in the morning (dictated by Der Hayr) to celebrate mass, perform a requiem service, or some other religious ceremony. The Der Hayr would make arrangements for a "backroom" at some rooming house, and Avedis would be required to assist as a deacon in the service. The two would recite their supplications, and then tearfully depart in the dark during the early morning hours.

Avedis, as forlorn as he was, tried to discourage the priest from such meetings but the Der Hayr was adamant. If Avedis were not available, Der Hayr Sahagian would recruit another Efkeretsi to serve as his deacon. Sadly, but predictably, a short time later, the young, troubled and disconsolate priest perished. He died years before his allotted time here on earth had expired. He was exterminated as surely as his compatriots were in Efkere.

Even six thousand miles away from the sites of those cruelties and crimes against mankind, Der Hayr Sahagian could not distance himself and escape the maddening terrors to save his sanity. In spite of his religious fervor and strength, that noble man of the cloth, gentle and caring, could not ward off the recurring nightmares of his sleepless nights.

Such was the depth and scope of the genocide of 1915. Its' horrors cursed an entire generation and its' residue lingers on. My generation became the children of 500,000 orphans. Time passed, and somehow Avedis struggled to carry on.

We don't know what happened to Avedis' restaurant or boarding house. We do know that some time in 1920 (he was now almost 30 years old), Avedis was encouraged by friends to go into the fur business. Some of his kinsmen and neighbors in Brooklyn had become furriers. They helped Avedis enter the Fur Workers Union and get a job with a company called Brooklyn Better Bleach, which was located in Jersey City, New Jersey.

Chapter 11

The Genocide Terrorizes the Sergenians

Returning to the story of my mother and her family, I will take you back to Tokat during the early spring of 1915. The situation between the Turks and Armenians was worsening. The directors of the Jesuit school of Tokat had decided to close the school and evacuate to their seminary in Constantinople. The Jesuit teachers, impressed with the young student Kaloust, now sixteen years old, persuaded him to come with them, disguised as a Catholic priest. Kaloust agreed, but first made every effort to convince the school to also bring his brother Souren to the safety of the "Bolis" (Constantinople as it was then called, Istanbul as it is now called) monastery. Unfortunately, Souren was still very young, just about eleven years old, and small in stature. Disguising him as a priest would endanger the entire contingent of Jesuit priests. Souren was left behind.

In the spring of 1915, Aghavni took her brother Souren to her home. Shortly thereafter, Aghavni's young husband was either forced into Turkish military service or taken "prisoner" with other young Armenians (on Turkish work details) and murdered. In 1914-1915, the Turks systematically "absorbed" young Armenian boys into the military. Thereupon, they would gather them into groups and execute these youngsters. This was their answer to the "Armenian threat." It was a horrible, but efficient method of decimating the strength of their subject minority. Extermination and exportation was the ruthless scheme of the Young Turks.

At this point, Victoria left Tokat with her two children, Kevork and Seranoush, to return to Shabin Karahisar. She had received word that the Turks had jailed many Armenian men in Karahisar. Her husband was among those in prison. He would soon be slaughtered there along with hundreds of others. Victoria was also intent on finding Ardemis amidst the chaos of Karahisar. Andon was in America, probably planning to join the Armenian volunteers to fight Turkey with Antranik.

Aghavni was in Tokat, having just lost her husband. Souren, we believe, was living with her. When the orders for deportation (exile) were posted Aghavni and Souren were somehow separated. Souren was last seen by Ankin Sergenian, the youngest daughter of cousin Nishan. Souren was now about eleven years. Ankin, who was in Tokat, saw Souren along the road leading out of the city. Souren was either riding a donkey or helping others (offering transport on the donkey). This was the beginning of the death marches in June of 1915.

Aghavni avoided deportation by fleeing to the hills. My mother (Ardemis) believed she lived with a Kurdish or Turkish woman (perhaps a hannum), who hid her and saved her from the death marches. Aghavni's daughter, Arouse, however, relates her mother's tale that Aghavni hid in the mountains and hills for almost three years. Whatever the case, her survival was nothing less than a miracle.

Kaloust, almost 17, with his bright intellect was selected by the Jesuits to train for the priesthood. He traveled with the Tokat Jesuit School across Turkey to Constantinople and the safety of the Catholic seminary.

Ardemis was living with her mother-in-law in Tamzara just 2 miles north of Karahisar. When the order for the deportations was issued, she fled to her aunt's home in Shabin Karahisar. She was determined to join the rallying call, "to the Pert," where armed resistance would take place. However, her sister Victoria arrived with her children and that notion of fighting on the "Pert" was quickly dismissed.

Chapter 12

The Death March

A. The Defense of Shabin Karahisar

During the late spring days of 1915, the political climate in Shabin Karahisar was heating up. Word had spread about atrocities committed against entire Armenian villages. News of wholesale public hangings in Constantinople of Armenian intellectuals circulated throughout Anatolia. Armenians everywhere were being exiled, forced from their homes and villages to undetermined destinations. [13]

"[T]he procedure was exceedingly systematic. The whole Armenian population of each town or village was cleared out, by a house-to-house search. Every [Armenian] was driven into the street. Some of the men were thrown into prison, where they were put to death, sometimes with torture; the rest of

the men, with women and children, were marched out of town. When they had got some little distance they were separated, the men being taken to some place among the hills where the soldiers, or the Kurdish tribes who were called in to help in the work of slaughter, dispatched them by shooting or bayoneting.

The women and children and old men were sent off under convoy of the lowest kind of soldiers- many of them just drawn from the gaols- to their distant destination, which was sometimes one of the unhealthy districts in the centre of Asia Minor, but more frequently the large desert in the province of Der el Zor, which lies east of Aleppo in the direction of the Euphrates. They were driven along by the soldiers day after day, all on foot, beaten or left behind to perish if they could not keep up with the caravan; many fell by the way, and many died of hunger. No provisions were given to them by the Turkish Government, and they had already been robbed of everything they possessed. Not a few of the women were stripped naked and made to travel in that condition beneath a burning sun. Some of the mothers went mad and threw away their children being unable to carry them further. The caravan route was marked by a line of corpses, and comparatively few seem to have arrived at the destinations which had been prescribed for them, - chosen, no doubt, because return was impossible and because there was little prospect that any would survive their hardships." [14]

The five to six thousand of what remained of the seven thousand Armenians in Karahisar were making their own preparations. Abdul Hamid's bloodletting and slaughter during every decade of his reign had taught the Armenians to remain vigilant. Few, if any, young men were left in Karahisar. Those who were not conscripted and sent away were being "detained in camps," or consigned to prisons. The older men, the women and children who inhabited the Armenian Wards along the slopes of the Fortress Mountain were aware of Ottoman treachery and were preparing to defend themselves and their homeland.

Interaction between the Turks and Armenians resulted in increasing incidents of hostility, oppression, and violence. Battle lines were being drawn. One could sense the impending cataclysm. Finally the rage on the mountain exploded. Shots were fired, individual battles broke out. As the Turkish troops assembled and encircled the Wards, the brave Armenian population of Karahisar rallied to the call "To the Fort, (Pert), it's time to fight!!!"

Although ownership of any kind of arms by Armenians was strictly forbidden and punishable by death, history led the spirited men of Karahisar to maintain munitions for use in self-defense. During the dark of night on an early June evening more than 5000 men, women and children gathered their basic needs, (guns, ammunition, knives, food, water and clothing), and climbed the precipitous mountain trail to the ancient fort. Many burned their homes rather than leave anything behind for the Turks. Most did not expect to return.

Many of this generation had experienced the massacres of the Red (as in bloody red) Sultan Abdul Hamid, in 1895.[15] Their path was clear. They were determined to defend themselves, their families, their church, and their culture to the death. One month later, after resisting the constant bombardment of a Turkish battalion which included heavy artillery, a starved, dehydrated and battered group of Armenians, mostly women and children, resisted no more. Barely 50 souls survived their month in Hell. More than 5000 of their kin had died in heroic defense of Shabin Karahisar.

Among those who took flight to the Pert to battle the Turks was "Uncle" Nishan Sergenian, whom we believe to be a first cousin, one generation removed to Sarkis (now dead some eight years). Nishan was a man with some political influence in Shabin Karahisar. He had a close personal relationship with the mayor. Upon the onset of the fighting, Nishan fled to the "Pert" with his family, which included daughters Seranoush, Haigouhi, Mentouhi and his son Mardiros. Two other daughters, Arshaluis and Ankin did not make the trek. I believe they were in Tokat.

Arshaluis' son, Gaidzak was among a number of Sergenian children to bear the terror of the mountain siege. Arshaluis had recently given birth to twins and was unable to make the strenuous climb. Haigouhi, who was pregnant, miscarried on the mountain. Arshaluis was later forced on the Shabin Karahisar death march with Ankin. She lost her twins during the journey. Starvation and disease gave no leeway to infants. During the battle on the "Pert," when the outcome became evident and suffering was no longer bearable, Uncle Nishan met with and attempted to negotiate a truce with the Turkish commander. His bloodied pocket-watch was sent back to his children as a sign of "Turkish Mercy!"

Amazingly, and miraculously, the remnants of cousin Nishan's family survived. They were among the 50 from the original 5000 that lived though that holocaust. Not only did they live, but were able to obtain papers from the mayor that effected safe passage for them through the hellish days. In time, they would all reunite in America with the four surviving children of Sarkis and Anna Sergenian.

Along with the three other valiant defensive struggles of Urfa, Van and Musa Dagh, this month long epic battle on the "Pert" would inspire Armenians everywhere. The deeds of these heroic people would become legend in poem and song. Their sacrifice would become a symbol of fearless bravery and courage. "The Pert" would no longer be referred to as just a place, or a mountain structure. But forever more it will be a heroic event. The deeds of those martyred 5000 will live on, emblazoned into the annals of Armenian History. Today, in Turkey, the Pert remains a sacred altar where those Armenian souls will eternally soar above the fallen Aerie.

B. Genocide: Turkish Style

By command of a wartime military decree, all people of Armenian ancestry were ordered to appear, at a given time, date and place, for relocation into a designated non-military zone. There would be absolutely no exceptions. Those in ill health, the aged, newborns, the blind, crippled, or pregnant were not excused.[16] Failure to assemble as directed was punishable by death. All personal goods, animals, etc. were to remain in their homes. Armenians were told that their homes, businesses, farms, and other property would to be safeguarded by the Turkish Army until the military action (World War I) was concluded, and then the exiles would be returned to their homes, and would be free to re-establish their lives as before. Exiles were permitted to take with them only that which could be carried by hand. The gendarmes protecting them would provide all other necessities at roadside.

Throughout the cities, towns and villages in all of Ottoman Turkey this scene was re-enacted. In only four locations did organized resistance and conflict take place: in Van, Musa Dagh, Urfa, and Shabin Karahisar. These events, which took place from 1915 through 1918 gave birth to the western newspapers phrase, "The Starving Armenians." That expression described perfectly the tattered remnants of a proud people. Unfortunately, it did little to provide an effective universal protest, and possibly an intercession to the ongoing mass execution of more than a million innocents.

Approximately three million Armenians were uprooted and scattered to the winds. This was the entire population of Armenians living in Turkey in 1915.[17] In many instances, especially in big cities where large populations of exiles were difficult to control, thousands were quickly mass slaughtered just outside the city gates. The Turks wanted no survivors or witnesses. Their "cleansing" needed to be perfect and complete. [18]

Decaying roadside corpses of the Armenian aged, women and children left undeniable evidence of mass murder. In this time and place of limited technology it was impossible to rid the pathways of the carnage they had perpetrated. Foreign ambassadors took note of the horrors being committed. Some Protestant and Catholic relief organizations made efforts to save the orphaned children. Little would be done to save their parents, grandparents or older siblings. The reign of terror continued on, in one way or another, for years. Genocide was widely reported by the world press. Many nations had eyes, but all lacked a conscience.

In many of the smaller villages and towns the Turks used a less violent, but quite effective variation to the march to exile. Simply by denying rest, food, water and shelter, the exiles would succumb to exhaustion, collapse and die. Families were urged to bury their dead. The evidence was thus, safely secreted. Death, the Turks said, was then just a "natural occurrence."

It is important to remember that the subjects of these marches were void of any self-protection. The younger Armenian men, ages 15 to 40 had already been conscripted into the military and were "disposed of" prior to the announcement of "relocation."[19] The older men of the village were usually "culled out" by the police and gendarmes and relocated separately. In most cases they were murdered in prison. The remainder or the majority of the deportees were women, children and the very elderly. They were defenseless. The refugees were forced to march to the south towards the wastelands and desserts of Syria, Iran and Iraq.

Nothing was provided for these desolate groups. "'Pray for us,' they would say as they left their homes; the land on which their ancestors had lived for 2500 years. 'We shall not see you in this world again, but sometime we shall meet. Pray for us.'" [20] The lines of the deported numbered as few as a hundred souls and as many as thousands. Just a handful would reach their elusive destination. Those who had gold or silver, jewels or currency could attempt to barter, but such attempts usually resulted in murder. The struggle to remain alive was almost hopeless.

Children were given away in desperation to Kurds or Turks because their outcome was preordained. It was starvation and death. Eyewitness Robert Morgenthau, United States Ambassador to Turkey noted with horror,

> *"Thus, in a few days, what had been a procession of normal human beings became a stumbling horde of dust-covered skeletons, ravenously looking for scraps of food, eating any offal that came their way, crazed by the hideous sights that had filled their very hours of existence, sick with all the diseases that accompany such hardships and privations, but still prodded on and on by the whips and clubs and bayonets of their executioners.* "[21]

Suicide was commonplace, and the rape and abduction of girls and young women was a daily (or nightly) event. Armenian girls were sold into a lifetime of servitude as concubines to the Turks. The refugees sustained themselves by eating anything they could find. Berries, roots, bark, and garbage was their food; and rain, the lakes, ponds and rivers was their water. Disease was their companion. The infants and very elderly died quickly as starvation and disease ravaged their ranks.

The waters of the Euphrates and Tigris rivers carried the bloated bodies of the starved and diseased, of the murdered and the self-destructed. "The most terrible scenes took place at the rivers, especially the Euphrates…In a loop of the river near Erzinghan, the thousands of dead bodies created such a barrage that the Euphrates changed its course for about a hundred yards."[22]   The only escape from their unholy genocide was the occasional "kidnapping" of the young. Some children would go willingly. All stolen or "adopted" children would be convinced to convert to the Islamic faith, and live the rest of their lives as slaves of their benefactors.

Babies who were given away by despondent mothers would never know their true ancestry. At the campsites, after completing a march of hundreds of miles, the few bedraggled survivors reaped their rewards. It was usually death by the sword, and finally, mass burial in the desserts and caves of southern Anatolia. It was completed. Turkey had been scoured of their Armenian subject people.

C.   Ardemis and Victoria on a March to Death: June - July 1915

70

Ardemis Sergenian Balian, just 13 years old, left her mother-in-law's home in Tamzara in late May 1915. She had heard rumors that her young husband Hampartsum had escaped from the Turkish army and was attempting to join the growing resistance in Karahisar.

Ardemis went to her Aunt Hripsime's home in Shabin Karahisar, determined to be a part of the defense along with her aunt's family. She believed all the Armenians would rally to the "Pert" and fight. She had hopes of a reunion with Hampartsum at the Fort and there they would all make their stand. Karahisar was in bedlam, and upon arriving she learned that her aunt's husband and their grown children had all been slain. Hripsimeh was grief stricken.

Aunt Hripsimeh had refused to allow her young niece to join the rush to the "Pert." The following day, Victoria arrived with her two young children. Soon thereafter, Ardemis and Victoria got news that the Turks had killed both their husbands. Hripsimeh urged her nieces and the children to flee to the relative safety of the Balian home in Tamzara. The girls reluctantly agreed. They had few other options and as for Aunt Hripsimeh, it is believed she made the trek alone up to the "Pert," and joined the thousands in the roll call of Armenian martyrdom.

When the siege of the citadel began, the two sisters and the two children were in Tamzara alone and terrified. Almost immediately after the start of battle, the local Turkish gendarmes assembled all the Armenians of Tamzara into two groups of two hundred and fifty people each. They were herded into the courtyards of the two Armenian churches. I believe Soorp Kevork was the larger church, and where my mother Ardemis and her sister Victoria began their march.

Victoria Sergenian, 23 years old, her children, Kevork, 5 years old, and Seranoush, 2 years old, began their forced march out of Tamzara with Ardemis, age 13, during the first days of June 1915. Guarded by Turkish and Kurdish "irregulars," (not much more than brigands and bandits), the groups were marched southward for "deportation" or as stated by the Ottoman government, "for temporary relocation." Victoria and Ardemis had no money, gold or jewelry with them. They managed to bring along some bread, cheese, nuts, extra clothing and shoes. They were permitted only that which they could carry. The journey was to be made on foot.

The account of my mother's forced march is similar to thousands of other "excursions to death," suffered by the Armenian people. These "Death Marches" were not local or isolated incidents, but rather, the careful fulfillment of a directive sent from the highest Turkish political and military offices throughout Anatolia. The infamous "Young Turks" had planned Genocide and had conceived the method, the structure and the rules governing their "final answer to the Armenian Question."

Except for sporadic help from a few compassionate Kurds, or even Turks, (aiding an Armenian was now severely punishable by Turkish law), this satanically devised vision of human annihilation resulted in the effective extermination of the Armenian nation from its ancestral soil. Never again would two to three million Armenians live in Historic Armenia.

My mother's group marched for about five weeks. The road they traveled was mountainous, but fortunately for them, they walked down from the mountains towards the plains around the Euphrates River and towards the basin of Lake Hazar. Each evening Victoria would hide and protect Ardemis, a very vulnerable 13 year old, by spreading all of their extra clothing upon her, and placing the two children on top of the pile.

Nightly raids by Kurds and sometimes Turks depleted the group of young teenage boys (as slave workers) and young teenage girls (for a more degrading manner of enslavement). They ate and drank whatever they could find, and whenever they could. They huddled at night and slept in the open, always aware of impending mayhem, kidnapping, rape or death.

When the two groups of Armenians reached Agin, about one hundred miles south of Shabin Karahisar, only thirty of the five hundred Tamzaratsis remained alive. Death by starvation, murder, and kidnapping had taken a terrible toll. The "camp" was probably a rest stop, a respite for the soldiers who were guarding the small tattered, half-alive contingent that remained.

Ardemis tearfully shared how they were encamped along the banks of the rushing waters of the Euphrates River. Neither shelter nor food was provided for the Armenians. The river, a ghastly, watery expressway for murdered and suicidal Armenians, provided the only drinking water. Its flow downstream offered a mournful parcel of bloated corpses and mutilated body parts, which gave testimony to the extent and depth of this genocide. Many survivors who witnessed this scene said the "river ran red with the blood of Armenians."

My mother recounted how on land, ravenous packs of wild dogs raided and scavenged the campsites after dark. The beasts would satisfy their hunger by devouring the dead and near dead. Screams and moans echoed pitifully throughout the night. At daybreak the remnants of shredded human remains gave proof to the horrific events of the evening past. This drama was truly a reenactment of the Satan's inferno, a journey into hell itself.

After a few days at Camp Agin, a Turkish lady of social and political status (a "Hannum") visited the site. She was in search of a good young girl whom she would extricate from this Hell and take to her home. There she would be trained as a servant, a handmaiden.

Of course the Hannum had with her the official papers needed to affect a release. The Hannum selected the pale, frightened and emaciated Ardemis. Terror stricken, Ardemis refused to leave her sister, Victoria. The Hannum shrewdly convinced Victoria to persuade Ardemis to accept her offer.

Victoria realized that this was a rare opportunity for Ardemis to escape starvation, degradation and eventual death. It was a chance for survival. After much prodding and pleading, Ardemis agreed to go, but only after the Hannum indicated the possibility of sending for Victoria at a later date.

At the Hannum's home in Agin (a palatial three story building), Ardemis met the rest of the staff. There were, surprisingly, nine other Armenians serving in varying capacities. The head cook was Armenian, as were the maids, carpet makers, and field workers. It appeared the Hannum had "a thing" for Armenian servants. The Armenian servants served without pay and were basically slaves. At least they were alive. During her stay, Ardemis constantly reminded the Hannum of her pledge to bring Victoria into the household as an assistant cook. Ardemis carefully never mentioned the children Kevork and Seranoush. The Hannum had not seen the two youngsters at the camp. Had she known of them she would never have agreed to take Victoria. Finally the Hannum obtained the extrication papers to release Victoria, and happily, Ardemis and the Armenian cook went to the camp.

At the campsite, the two searched in vain. Eventually they were told that Victoria, realizing her situation was hopeless (certainly no one would take on an Armenian woman as a servant as long as she had her own infants in her care), had made the final decision of her life. Just a day earlier, despondent and near starvation, she held her two beloved angels to her breast and committed all three souls into the hands of God. Victoria threw herself into the raging Euphrates, inhaled its' waters, and joined the countless scores who chose martyrdom. Victoria accepted death not because she hated life, but because she so loved life, and she could no longer bear to see it so defiled.

Ardemis was inconsolable. She wailed and cried hysterically. Her guilt was almost as great as her grief. She felt she had abandoned her sister and children in a trade of their lives for hers. Her only thoughts were now to follow her sister's actions. Those around her thwarted her attempts. After some time, the Hannum's Armenian cook and some of the exiles helped to calm and comfort the emotionally crushed child.

Ardemis was overwhelmed with her loss and this moment in time would spawn a nightmare that would haunt her for the rest of her life. With gentle and genuine compassion, the Armenians around Ardemis suggested that perhaps Victoria had feigned drowning to escape the guards and the camp. Further, they commented that Ardemis needed to gain strength and carry on in order to find and be reunited with her family again.

Although distraught and weak, Ardemis finally agreed to return to the home of the Hannum. The summer of 1915 had been a defining period in the life Ardemis Sergenian. She had lost her family in Tokat. She would never again see her closest playmate, her beloved brother Souren. She was informed of the death of uncles, cousins, and her brother-in-law, and even the husband she never really knew. She had witnessed the flight to the "Pert" by heroic, but doomed Karahisaritzes. She had been herded and driven, as cattle to the slaughter. She had experienced thirst, hunger, fear, degradation, and only God knows what else, in order to survive. She saw death often and up close.

She had been plucked out, as a lamb from a pen, to escape her own death, but only to experience depression in the deepest and darkest abyss. With the loss of her oldest sister and little niece and nephew, Ardemis was consumed with the full and final weight of being totally alone, an orphan. She said, at this point she failed to live. She only functioned as in a dream. The pale skinned teenager had been inducted into the army of the living dead.

Chapter 13

Ardemis and the Hannum

After Ardemis' return to the home of the Hannum, she resumed her assigned duties. As in a trance she helped the cook in the kitchen, washed and ironed clothes, cleaned house and picked fruit and tended the garden. At night she slept in a small room on the second floor where the carpet loom was maintained. Ardemis shared the room with two other Armenian servant girls. In time, she developed a close relationship with one of the girls. Her first name was Pekrouhi. I'm not aware if this name was her birth name, or a Turkish assigned name.

One day, while working in the gardens, Ardemis and Pekrouhi found a few torn pages of an Armenian Bible. The girls secreted their find, and clandestinely read and re-read the pages at night, by candlelight. At about the same time, the uncle of the

Hannum, who was an important official in the Agin government directed the Hannum to convert her Armenian servants to Islam.

Ardemis was given no choice but to sign official papers that stated that she was now a Turkish Moslem. Her duties were expanded to the study of the Koran and to further her ability to read and write in the Islamic Turkish tongue. Her name was no longer Ardemis, but Pekar.

Pekar and her fellow servant Pekrouhi became close friends. Besides reading the Armenian Bible under the cover of night, the two spoke the forbidden language of Armenian to each other. Many years later, Ardemis learned that Pekrouhi had also escaped from the yoke of the Hannum and made her way to America. She was actually living nearby, in the Philadelphia area. However, the two companions in exile never did renew their friendship in the United States. Perhaps reliving the memories of those days would be too painful.

The Hannum had three children. The eldest was an eighteen-year-old daughter. In addition, she had a thirteen-year-old daughter and an eight-year-old son. The two youngest children paid little attention to the servants, but the eighteen-year-old, testing her growing maturity and authority, was abusive and cruel. The Armenian girls avoided her whenever possible. On the other hand, the Hannum was strict but fair. She demonstrated both civility and consideration for her help.

Ardemis, it appears, was one of the Hannum's favorites. The warm regard the mistress held for her fair skinned Armenian maid probably resulted in Ardemis' flight to freedom some years later in 1918. The Hannum's husband had been an influential political figure. He was the chief secretary to a Pasha in Istanbul during the reign of the "Red Sultan" Abdul Hamid. When the "Young Turks" disposed of the sultan, the Hannum's husband sent his wife and three children from Istanbul to Agin (for their safety). During the course of World War I, the husband remained in Istanbul. Perhaps he worked for the new Ottoman government during the war. In the early months of 1918, as the war was reaching its conclusion, the husband's intention was to reunite with his family in Istanbul. He wrote the Hannum and instructed her to prepare for the journey back to their home in Istanbul.

The Hannum, her two daughters, now twenty-one and sixteen years old, and her son, eleven years old, departed for the Black Sea Port of Geresun. With them, the Hannum "invited" three of her Armenian servant girls, Ardemis (Pekar), Pekrouhi, and Arshalious. Ardemis was told before setting out that she was chosen to accompany and serve the elder daughter after the young woman was married in Istanbul. It appeared to be a reward. Some reward!

Giresun is situated on the banks of the Black Sea between Ordu to the west and Trebizond on the east. It is located almost two hundred miles due north of Agin and seventy miles north of Shabin Karahisar.

The Hannum and her family rode horses (perhaps on a wagon called an "araba "), while the servants walked. The journey north into the Pontus Mountains, started in April of 1918. It retraced the footsteps, where Victoria and Ardemis had suffered so terribly, three years earlier. The mountainous trek toward the Black Sea must have taken months. It was an arduous climb into the high country of Ardemis' homeland. It was a return to the land of the "Eagle's Aerie." When the group reached the outskirts of Shabin Karahisar, the Hannum recalled that the village was Ardemis' birthplace. Consolingly and perhaps innocently, the Hannum asked Ardemis if she wished to visit with any of her family before the group pushed on to Giresun.

Ardemis, guessing the worst in what befell the fate of her sisters and brothers declined. The sixteen year old was also fear stricken of the sadistic police chief of Karahisar. "If he knew I was a Karahisartsi, he would surely jail or execute me." Ardemis' terror ran deep. After all, this was the city of the revolt, and the Turks hated no one more than the rebellious Armenians.

After a few more weeks of mountain travel, the Hannum and her charges reached Giresun. There, the Hannum received instructions from her husband not to depart (by ship) until the armistice had been signed. The group passed the rest of the summer and early fall in the attractive seaport city. In November of 1918 the war ended, and the Hannum made arrangements to sail for Istanbul. On board ship, Hannum and her children had staterooms, but the three Armenian girls were relegated to travel in "steerage" class and slept at nights on the bare floor in the lowest compartment of the ship. The girls continued to serve the family during the voyage.

After a few days Ardemis became friendly with a Greek woman who was sailing to Bulgaria with her two children. The woman spoke Turkish, and gently coaxed Ardemis to tell her tale. Horrid stories about the sufferings of Armenians, especially young girls, were prevalent during these days. I'm certain the Greek woman had suspicions about young Ardemis' enslavement. The Greek lady was so moved by the young Armenian's story she hid Ardemis in her own room for two days and nights. She hoped to rescue Ardemis by taking her to Bulgaria (the next port after Constantinople), and making her a member of her own family. However, Ardemis explained to her that she believed she had family, a brother Kaloust, in Constantinople at the Jesuit school (seminary).

Thereupon, the Greek woman planned an escape for Ardemis. She conspired with a Greek cook on board who was familiar with Bolis and even knew where a nearby Armenian Church was located. He volunteered to attempt to bring aid from the church. The plan was for the cook to leave the ship immediately after docking and go for help. The following morning (the ship stayed in port for two days), Ardemis would sneak off. With fearful concern, the Greek woman, the cook and Ardemis were certain the Hannum would try to find and reclaim her.

When the time came for her flight to freedom, Ardemis was given a large scarf to cover her shoulders, and hide her head and face. The Greek told her to speak to no one, but go directly to a rope ladder, not the gangplank, and climb down. They hoped help would be waiting at dockside.

After the precarious climb down, Ardemis was elated to see the cook with a member of the Board of Trustees of the neighborhood Armenian Church. But their worst fears were soon realized as the Hannum and her husband came running to confront them. The Hannum had disembarked the previous day, and with the support of her husband had searched the ship. Now she was waiting dockside for just such an escape effort. The two Turks were furious, but the Armenian Church Board member was resolute in saving the frightened Ardemis. Police were finally called (French Police because the Turks had lost the war to the Allies). The decision was made to take the case to the courts.

At the courthouse the Hannum approached Ardemis and asked why she fled. Ardemis began to tell of her brother Kaloust, but was quickly silenced by the Board member not to reveal any information.

Before the judge the Hannum explained that she had signed papers from Ardemis who was now a Moslem and her ward. The judge then asked Ardemis about her situation. How did Ardemis come to work for the Hannum, and did she willingly convert to Islam? Ardemis explained that she had no choice but to accept and work for the Hannum, and was forced to sign the paper converting her to Islam. She explained that she had a brother in Bolis, and wanted to be reunited with him. The judge thereupon told Ardemis she was free to go with the Board member and that the Hannum's family no longer had any claims on her.

The Hannum's last words to her favorite servant were "Pekar, I thought you would never leave us." It appears it was a bittersweet parting for the Hannum. She was of course aware that she had saved Ardemis' life, and was responsible for her welfare. She expected gratitude and servitude with loyalty in return. Her Pekar was gone. Ardemis was free.

Chapter 14

A Miracle in Constantinople: 1918 and Onward

It was late November of 1918. Ardemis Sergenian was sixteen and a half years old in the great metropolis of Constantinople. After the judge decreed that the Hannum had no rights or privileges concerning the life of Ardemis, the teenager was escorted directly to the Armenian Church. As the Turks had lost the war and surrendered there was an air of submissive chaos. The Allies, especially the French, ruled the post-war bedlam.

Although crushed by the devastation of the Genocide the few surviving Armenians in Bolis were frantically attempting to put their lives in order. Confusion was the state of the community. At the church, Ardemis was queried at length about the events in her life in Shabin Karahisar, the Death

85

March and her three years of forced servitude with the Hannum. Ardemis tearfully recalled her story to the Trustees and pleadingly asked their help in locating her brother Kaloust who she believed was still at the Bolis Jesuit School. The Trustees told her they would make every effort to find Kaloust. The Trustees also told her that the Armenians on the boat from which she escaped were the first of the surviving exiles out of the interior since War's end.

After the interview, Ardemis felt weak and faint. She asked for a place to rest. Unbeknownst to her, she had contracted the dreaded Spanish Flu on the ship; the flu that would kill millions worldwide in 1918 and 1919. Ardemis, exhausted and feverish, slept as in a semi-coma for 2 or 3 days. The ladies at the church did what they could for her but this strain of flu was extremely virulent and tens of thousands died as the epidemic ravaged post war Constantinople.

In the meantime, the church Trustees tracked down Kaloust in a Jesuit seminary. Kaloust, along with hundreds perhaps thousands of other Armenians who had lost their families desperately searched everywhere for news of loved ones. Kaloust had even placed notices in newspapers, seeking any information. He prayed constantly for word from his sisters or brothers. His despair and loneliness was ingrained with pangs of guilt because of his inability to protect and save little brother Souren. Kaloust suffered much in same fashion as Ardemis, through her loss of Victoria, Kevork and Seranoush.

Kaloust was overjoyed to learn that his sister was alive and at the Armenian Church. He was told, however, that her health was precarious at best. Kaloust rushed immediately to her bedside. With amazement he gazed upon the semi-conscious Ardemis. He had expected to find his "strong" older sister, Aghavni; not his frail baby sister, Ardemis.

Kaloust, with the help of two friends, transported Ardemis by stretcher to his room at the seminary. A Jesuit priest, who was also a doctor, attended the delirious Ardemis, and admitted her into the Catholic hospital. During her two-month stay in a ward Ardemis would awaken from time-to-time to find the beds of adjoining patients suddenly empty. Again and again this hazy dream scene would occur. She was not told until she had fully recovered that most of the patients about her had died. The death rate of influenza patients was tragically high. Recovery was seen as almost a miracle.

During most of her stay at the hospital Ardemis had fleeting visions of brother Kaloust. It would be weeks before she realized that he was really there, caring for her and beseeching heaven for her recovery. When recognition finally occurred the brother and sister embraced. Though few tears were left in their souls, they were shed at this moment of reunion.

Ardemis' "guardian angel" had again touched the youngster with her saving grace. Ardemis had done it again. She had survived.

About the same time, in the city of Sivas (Sepastia), hundreds of miles east of Bolis, another drama was unfolding. A friend of Aghavni Sergenian read the search notice which Kaloust had placed in the paper. She showed the paper to Aghavni who immediately left for Constantinople. I am not certain how Aghavni had survived the massacres. My mother, Ardemis, told my sister that she believed Aghavni had gained refuge with another Hannum near Tokat, perhaps in Sepastia. Ardemis was unsure if Aghavni had escaped or the Hannum had released her.

Another version of Aghavni's tribulations comes from my cousin Arouse, Aghavni's daughter. Arouse recalls her mother's infrequent recollection of that five year period. Aghavni had escaped the "roundup" of the Tokat death march. She subsequently fled into the hills and mountains about the area. She banded together with several other Armenians and together they survived as wild animals, foraging for food and water. Aghavni stated that for 5 years she never experienced her monthly menstrual cycle. Even after the war had concluded, Aghavni and her compatriots avoided Tokat, their hometown. They still feared the wrath of the Ottoman murderers. Instead they walked to the provincial capital of Sivas. There they sought out other Armenians in the metropolis and began the search for family members.

In either scenario, Aghavni came to Constantinople from Sivas and found Kaloust. Together the two would visit Ardemis at the hospital. As one could expect, the two eventually contracted the Spanish Flu. Fortunately, their symptoms were less severe and they were soon out of the hospital.

After her lengthy recovery, Ardemis stayed at the hospital, working with the nuns. She made beds, served meals and did other menial tasks. She also learned a little Greek and French. The nuns saw the potential in Ardemis, and they approached her to join their order. Here the strong voice and iron will of big sister Aghavni took command.

Although grateful for the protection and care the Jesuits provided her siblings, Aghavni immediately extracted the vulnerable Ardemis from the confines of the hospital. She even vehemently advised Kaloust to leave the Jesuits. After all, he was baptized as an Armenian Apostolic. Kaloust remained for a short while with the order, but found an apartment near the seminary for his two sisters.

In the early spring of 1920, Andon Sergenian had been separated from Antranik's volunteer army. While living in Adana, in the Cilician region of Historic Armenia with many other Armenian refugees, he too saw his brother Kaloust's notice in an old issue of an Armenian language newspaper. He left for Bolis and remarkably four of the six Sergenian children were reunited.

Ardemis recounted none of the emotion of this final sibling reunion. Four together, and two lost forever. How much unspoken pain dimmed the gleam in their eyes? How much penetrating guilt wracked their beings for the rest of their lives. A formal family portrait was taken at a Constantinople photographer's studio to celebrate the event. How they all treasured each other's redemption. The four had been saved from the inferno, and were together again.

As unbelievable as the joyous occasion was, the brothers and sisters could (or would) only share brief and incomplete accounts of their personal trauma since they had separated. Ardemis, still withdrawn and taciturn, secreted to the deepest chambers of her heart and psyche the events that led to Victoria's and the children's self-imposed demise. Only, after some fifty years was she able to tearfully reveal to her sister Aghavni the truth about Victoria's fate in the Euphrates River of death. Both Kaloust and Andon were never told about Victoria's final days during that summer of 1915. Ardemis and the rest of us still do not know how Souren became separated from Aghavni. We only know of Ankin Sergenian's sighting of him during the first days of the Tokat death marches. We do not know if he managed to survive or was doomed to die in those terrible days of gross massacres.

After Andon arrived and completed the Sergenian reunion, Kaloust finally decided to leave the Jesuits. These men were not only his teachers; they were his saviors in the midst of genocide. Kaloust was a scholar in many disciplines, but especially in foreign languages. He was conversant in Armenian, Turkish, English, French, German, and Italian and could get by in Greek and Spanish.

The Sergenians had achieved the near impossible. The two brothers and two sisters had found each other in war torn Constantinople in 1920. They were, again, a family unit. Their lives gave testimony to a somber Armenian victory.

In Constantinople, Andon worked with fellow Karahisaritzes aiding incoming refugees from their home village, as well as other newly arrived Armenians. The group helped provide food, shelter, and jobs and tried diligently to reunite the scavenged and separated families. It was a heart-wrenching undertaking. Kaloust found employment in a large restaurant, and in a short period of time was elevated to headwaiter. Aghavni used her embroidery skills to provide income. However, her most significant contribution to the life of her family was soon to take place. Aghavni was told by a friend about a young Armenian man in America, who was searching for an Armenian bride. The young man, (actually he was now beyond his 30th birthday), was Mirijan Dermengian. Mirijan had been born in Sepastia, the youngest of 13 children, and the only one to survive.

He had been married as a youth in Sivas, and had quickly fathered a family of six children. When forced into military service and sent to the Balkans, Mirijan managed to escape and immigrate to America. His dream was to provide the means to bring his entire family to the United States. Turkey meant servitude and death, while America was the promise of freedom and life.

The Genocide destroyed his family as well as his dream. Now, five years later, he was attempting to rebuild his shattered life. A number of letters passed between Mirijan and Aghavni and photographs were exchanged. A copy of the photograph of Aghavni, which was sent to Mirijan, exists today in our family album. It shows the thin, stately Aghavni posing in a Constantinople photo studio. The 23-year-old is standing in an artificial garden setting, with her arm draped over a wicker chair.

An agreement was struck between the two, and plans for Aghavni's departure were formulated. It seems that the "picture bride" Aghavni agreed to marry Mirijan with the understanding that Mirijan would later help Aghavni's siblings to immigrate to America. This single event, driven by Aghavni's devotion and determination to save her family, was a most significant decision for all the surviving Sergenians.

In the fall of 1920 Aghavni bid farewell to Andon, Kaloust, and Ardemis. She sailed from

Constantinople, passed through Ellis Island and into the arms, (and wedding vows) of Mirijan Dermengian. In 1920 Mirijan lived in or about the city of Syracuse and was employed as a fireman in the fire pits of the Hood Rubber Company. He traveled to New York City to greet Aghavni (with a chaperon) and the two were married on January 8, 1921. It was Aghavni's good fortune to find a wonderful man such as Mirijan. Their union changed the lives of all the Sergenian children.

As for Mirijan, he was truly a generous and loving man. He was a warmly gentle and happy person who loved all, and was loved by all. His disposition was almost the opposite of his spouse Aghavni, who was fiercely intense, single-minded and focused, and profoundly protective of family. "The Killing Fields" of Tokat and Shabin Karahisar had toughened Aghavni with the resolve of a "fediyheen" (freedom fighter).

Together Mirijan and Aghavni complimented each other's virtues and diminished each other's faults. They were a perfect match, a classic example of opposites attracting. After Aghavni sailed for America, the remaining Sergenians continued their lives in Constantinople. Since Turkey was a defeated nation of World War I, the French occupation forces had control of most government functions. The Armenian refugees who flooded the city were at least consoled by the Allied victory. Of course, the terrors of the past would never permit a survivor to trust a

Turk or call one a friend. I believe Constantinople had become the central transient stop for what were called "the wandering Armenians." Few would remain there. Through the ensuing years, the refugees of Anatolia scattered throughout the world. It was the start of the Diaspora for our people. Of all the prospective nations, America was the golden destination. The Sergenians just bided their time.

In the fall of 1920, Ardemis was working at what she described as the "Bible House," producing with painstaking care and precision, the hand works that were known as "Aintab Embroideries." In February of 1921, shortly after Aghavni and Mirijan's wedding, Ardemis, Kaloust and Andon received $500.00 from Aghavni and Mirijan. Aghavni had kept her promise. The funds (it was a fortune in those days) for a chance of a new life had arrived.

The money was meant to buy steamship passage to America, and to provide in cash the fifty dollars lawfully necessary for each immigrant to pass through the gates of Ellis Island.

A. <u>Andon</u>

Andon, now the oldest surviving Sergenian, (he was almost 27 years old), had made different plans. During the past decade Andon, with help from family members, and his own remarkable resourcefulness, had already made two sojourns to America. Prior to his mother's death in 1912, Andon had been subject to Turkish conscription law. All

94

Armenians realized that, for them, military duty was akin to a death sentence. Young Armenians used every means available to escape service. Andon's relatives provided him with the money to travel to America and to escape Turkish service.

Andon kept in touch with his family while living in Philadelphia. When he learned that it was safe to return, he did so. His stay in Shabin Karahisar, however, was short lived. The Ottomans again conscripted all available Armenian youth, and again Andon found the means to flee to America. Andon was in America when World War I broke out and when the word of the Armenian Genocide spread across the pages of the New York Times. Andon joined a contingent of the French Foreign Legion comprised solely of Armenians that was destined to fight Turkey. Somehow, he was able to find his way to Antranik's volunteer army, and fought side by side with his countrymen until the war's end.[23]

During their stay in Constantinople, Andon showed that he was considerably more sophisticated, worldly and street wise than his siblings. Kaloust, from childhood, had lived a cloistered life at the Jesuit school. Ardemis, despite her survival of the perilous days from 1915 through 1918, was a stranger to the mysteries, delights and dangers of big city life. She was amazed at all she saw in Constantinople.

Even her first experience with the simple banana was a marvel. She had never seen such a strange and exotic fruit. She had to be shown how to peel it so she could eat it. Andon on the other hand, had acquired city smarts. Although his academics were not as extensive or varied as brother Kaloust's (both trained with Jesuits in Tokat), Andon was the indomitable free spirit. Unafraid of the unknown and willing to experience all of life, he was the adventurer of the clan.

When the money arrived from sister Aghavni, Andon decided not to return to America. He saw an opportunity to start a business in the new post-war Bolis. Andon took his share of the immigration money and started a business venture. He remained in Constantinople for a short time. Then, the struggle for political power in Turkey fell into the hands of Mustafa Kemal. The occupying French forces eventually left Anatolia when the new "Democratic Republic of Turkey" was born. The repression and killings of the Armenians began anew and Andon saw the futility of remaining in Turkey. In 1922, he left Turkey never to return.

Andon immigrated to Greece. There Andon met, courted and married Shushan Shahinian (also spelled Chahimian) a very young survivor from Van. In October of 1924 Andon and Shushan had a daughter, Annig, and shortly thereafter they left Greece and settled in Paris, France. In Paris, Andon founded and ran a leather goods factory where he manufactured shoes, handbags, and belts. The Andon Sergenians (he spelled his name Sardjenian) endured and persevered through the horrors of World

War II including the occupation of Paris by the Nazis.

At about this time, Souren, son of Aghavni and Mirijan, was serving in the United States Army and was severely wounded while fighting the Germans in the Battle of the Bulge. His recovery, in part, took place in Paris, at the home of Andon and Shushan. Here Souren met, fell in love with, and eventually married Annig, Andon's and Shushan's daughter. At war's end, Souren brought Annig home to America.

As for Andon, after the Armistice in 1945, he began to exhibit his wide range of talents by writing and lecturing on his own concepts regarding health, philosophy and metaphysics. His teachings and treatise were published in both English and French under his pen name "The Naturalist Andon." In 1950, Andon and Shushan immigrated to America. After a short stay on the East Coast, they settled in California. Their home was close to Annig and Souren, and sister Aghavni and her husband Mirijan, (the Dermengians had all left Syracuse New York a few years earlier).

Andon and his beloved Shushan worked side by side creating ceramic craft pieces. Their life was simple in America. They had moved close to their daughter Annig and son-in-law Souren in Southern California. Andon and Shushan found great joy in their grandchildren, whom they adored. Diane and John were bright and beautiful children, always a delight to their grandparents.

When Andon died in 1967, he was almost 74 years old. Shushan bravely survived until 1998. After Andon's death, Annig gave her mother her constant love and support. During the last few years of Shushan's life, she was a resident in a senior citizen nursing home. Annig was at her bedside daily to provide help and encouragement. Souren had died a few years previously, so the two women comforted each other. When Shushan passed in 1998, the final chapter of the Sergenian siblings and their spouses was completed.

Chapter 15

America: 1921

Some time in late winter, or early spring of 1921, Ardemis and Kaloust said their farewells to Andon and departed on a Turkish ship bound for Piraeus, Greece. Their next booking had them traveling aboard the ship named the "King Alexander," to New York City. Unfortunately, the King Alexander had broken down and was harbored somewhere in France undergoing extensive repairs.

The steamship line rescheduled the crossing on a smaller ship, the "Megali Elas," but there was a departure delay of three weeks. The steamship carrier provided rooms in Piraeus during the wait, but meals and other personal expenses were not covered.

Kaloust had an insatiable thirst for knowledge and armed with his outstanding and diverse linguistic skills was thrilled at the prospect of exploring

Greece. He journeyed to Athens, and rediscovered the home of Plato, Aristotle and Homer. He was careful not to spend too much of his money so he most likely slept in the open and ate sparingly. Ardemis, meanwhile, remained confined in her hotel room. She was, by her own words, "so afraid" that her brother would not conserve the necessary $50.00 to "enter" America. In fact, she decided to sew her "entrance money" into her undergarments, while awaiting Kaloust's return from Athens.

In late April of 1921, Ardemis and Kaloust boarded the Megali Elas and sailed to America. The voyage was rough, and Kaloust suffered terribly with seasickness. Because of their meager funds, Ardemis and Kaloust could only afford steerage class accommodations. Uncomfortable, to be sure, but they were on the way.

Among the passengers, Ardemis and Kaloust met a young man from their hometown of Shabin Karahisar. The three young adults sadly recounted how they had escaped the Genocide, and with great joy, how they looked forward to America. The young man was Aram Haigaz, who at the age of 13 (exactly Ardemis' age) had fought on the "Pert." Some years later in the 1930's, Aram Haigaz wrote the unforgettable tale of survival called Fall of the Aerie. It was a comprehensive, historic depiction of the defense of Shabin Karahisar. The book was published in Boston in 1938, and later it was serialized in the Hairenik Daily Newspaper. Aram

Haigaz dedicated his book to the heroes of Shabin Karahisar. Aram was one of those heroes, both atop the Pert, and later, on our bookshelves and in our hearts.

As fate would have it, many years later an elderly Aram Haigaz found employment as a photoengraver with Dick and I, and our partners Mr. Edward Sahagian (an Efkeretsi as my Dad), and his son Eddie, and Sam Vosganian, another survivor of Shabin Karahisar. To me this was a remarkable melding of old world blood with new world business.[24]

Back on the ship, Ardemis and Kaloust were overjoyed at the sight of the Statue of Liberty greeting them as they entered New York Harbor on May 1, 1921. The crossing had taken nine days. Their passage through immigration was uneventful and the young brother and sister found themselves on the strange and exciting streets of New York City.

At this time, Aghavni and Mirijan were still living in upstate New York in Syracuse. Kaloust and Ardemis had to find a way to get to Syracuse. Using his language skills, Kaloust heard a stranger speaking German. He approached and asked the man for help. He was directed to Grand Central Station. There, Kaloust found the train to Syracuse.

As far as we know, the four, Aghavni, Mirijan, Kaloust and Ardemis, lived together in one apartment. When the Hood Rubber Company closed its' plant in Syracuse and Mirijan became unemployed, Kaloust and Ardemis had yet to find work. Aghavni took the initiative. Once again, she was a woman not to be denied. She returned by herself to New York City intent on finding work for the whole family, and she did.

So, after a short stay upstate, the Sergenians and Dermengians were back in New York City. The four shared a two-bedroom apartment on 26th Street and Third Avenue, just a few blocks from the newly consecrated St. Illuminators Armenian Apostolic Cathedral. Kaloust found work (and a new profession) with Sebouh Sergenian (a distant relative). He was introduced to the Oriental rug trade. He began by picking up, cleaning and delivering rugs. Soon he was doing repairs. Finally, he evaluated, bought and sold rugs.

As for Ardemis, she worked on consignment, at home, continuing to advance her skills in the delicate creation of Aintab motif embroideries. Aghavni worked outside the house, but we are not sure of her trade. Mirijan, through another friend, also entered the carpet and rug trade, where he worked for many years.

Chapter 16

Avedis Meets Ardemis and More: 1921-1930

L ate in the summer of 1921, the wife of Avedis'
close friend and fellow Efkeretsi, Hagop
Kalajian (Baron Hagop) told Avedis about a newly
arrived single Armenian girl. The Kalajians were
actively attempting to break Avedis out of the
depressing malaise which had engulfed him since
1915.

Mrs. Kalajian told Avedis that the young girl
was attractive, but shy and withdrawn. She had
endured a death march and had been interred in a
Turkish household for almost three years. Avedis
was still seeking answers to what had happened in
1915, and here seemed to be an opportunity to fill in
a few more gaps of this nightmarish tale that would

not let him rest. The young girl, who was barely 19, was Ardemis Sergenian.

Avedis, having obtained the address from Mrs. Kalajian, finally decided to call on Ardemis one weekday afternoon. Ardemis' apartment, which she shared with Kaloust, Aghavni and Mirijan, had a bathroom which they shared with the mother-in-law of Hagop Kalajian. Hence the connection for the introduction between Avedis and Ardemis.

The day Avedis came to visit Ardemis, Aghavni, Mirijan and Kaloust were at work. Ardemis was startled at the sight of a stranger at the door. She knew no one and was not expecting any visitors. Avedis introduced himself to the young Ardemis, and explained their mutual relationship with her Armenian neighbor. Ardemis invited him in and offered him a chair which Avedis discovered to be unsteady; in fact, it was broken. After a few uneasy moments the two sat at the kitchen table, and began to unfold their tragic stories to each other. Ardemis, now feeling comfortable with Avedis, offered him some coffee, but Avedis declined and accepted an apple instead. The two exchanged information about their previous marriages, their families and some details of their flight from Turkey to America. Toward the end of the afternoon Avedis took his leave, but expressed his desire to visit Ardemis again. Ardemis did not discourage him.

Inwardly, Avedis thought their age differences might be too great to consider a serious relationship.

Avedis was now almost 31, some twelve years older than Ardemis. However, he did continue to call, increasing his visits from two or three times a week to almost daily. In less than one month, Avedis proposed marriage to Ardemis.

Ardemis, although enamored with Avedis, told him that she would need the approval and blessings of her brother, sister and brother-in-law before considering the proposal. Ardemis informed the family of Avedis' intentions, and Kaloust and Aghavni decided to investigate the background, character and financial status of Avedis Sarajian.

Among others, they asked a cousin, Sebouh Sergenian, an "unger," (compatriot), of Avedis in the local political club for his opinion. Sebouh, when quizzed, spoke very highly of Avedis, whom he knew quite well. His one concern was their age difference. When confronted with the age problem, Ardemis openly expressed her love for Avedis, and convinced her brother and sister that the union was just what she wanted. Avedis arranged the wedding to take place on October 16, 1921 (his 31st birthday).

The ceremony was celebrated at St. Illuminator's Armenian Cathedral on East 27th Street in Manhattan. It was one of the first weddings ever to take place in the new Cathedral. Some 29 years later, in May of 1950, Avedis and Ardemis saw their son Dikran marry Arax Catchouny at the same alter. And then again, 41 years after their wedding, Avedis and Ardemis attended the marriage ceremony of their son Haig to Mary Kachian in their beloved St. Illuminators.

A few weeks before his wedding, Avedis had asked his young friend and fellow Efkeretsi Edward Sahagian to be his best man (Godfather). Edward was the youngest son of Der Hayr Sahagian. However Edward, now a university student, cited that he had little money, and could not in good conscience accept the responsibility of Godfather. Edward suggested Mr. Hagop Nergizian, a contemporary of Avedis' who was an Efkeretsi as well. Hagop Nergizian was a tailor with a shop in Harlem. Hagop, perhaps a few years older than Avedis, was a tall, graceful gentleman with close ties to Avedis. He happily accepted the role and responsibility of Godfather.

Since Baron Nergizian was widowed at the time, the place of Godmother (maid or matron of honor) was offered and accepted by Oijen Stepanian, another Efkeretsi. Custom dictated that the groom or his family would determine the selection of Godfather and Godmother. The bride had little or no say in this matter.

Ardemis' wedding gown was borrowed from a friend. Her sister Aghavni gave her wedding veil to her, and we believe her shoes were her own. A professional wedding picture was taken, and it is part of the family's collection of photographs. That wedding photograph appeared in the commemorative program celebrating St. Illuminator's 75th anniversary. A very small reception was held at the Stepanian household. Few of Ardemis' relatives and friends were invited. Was this custom again?

The newlyweds made their first home in an apartment at 118 Graton Street, Brooklyn, New York. Avedis and Ardemis enjoyed an abbreviated three-day honeymoon by going to vaudeville shows and movies, and dining at restaurants. In less than a year, their first son Dikran (Dick) was born on August 19, 1922. Shortly thereafter, Ardemis gave birth to their daughter, Mariam (Mary), on April 19, 1924.

In October of 1928, Ardemis, now married seven years gave birth to another son, Souren, named in memory of Ardemis' lost younger brother. But in less than six months heartbreak again struck Avedis and Ardemis. Tragically, in April 1929, Souren died of a childhood illness which we think was caused by complications from impetigo.

A little more than a year later on October 16, 1930, on Avedis' 40th birthday, and the couple's 9th wedding anniversary, Ardemis and Avedis' last child, Haig, was born.

Chapter 17

The Depression, War and Post War Years

A.   Avedis and Ardemis

Soon after Haig's birth, the terrible years of the Great Depression followed. Avedis lost his job as a furrier. The days of opulence, and fun of the "roaring 20's" had ended. Avedis struggled mightily and painfully to provide. At one time or another he sold apples on street corners, took photographs for pennies at Coney Island, and worked as a shoemaker.

But together with little more than love and determination, the family survived. In spite of all the indignities of the times, Avedis toiled and battled. After all, he had the love of his wife and children to support him, and he was a free man in America.

Avedis adored his family and his country. His relationship with his wife's family was also strong and loving. Avedis absorbed and returned the love of his wife's family almost as a replacement of his own murdered family. The new bonds which were forged in the early 20's actually strengthened in spite of the adversity of the depression. The family was together and they had learned to depend on each other.

As the depressing years of want passed, the Sergenians in America drifted apart geographically. First Kaloust and his family moved to Boston, and later in the 40's Aghavni, Mirijan and their family moved to California. After World War II, Andon and Shushan immigrated to the United States and after a short stay on the East Coast, they too settled in California.

During those same years Avedis and Ardemis also moved a number of times. From their first apartment on Graton Street, Avedis (it was always Avedis) found new living quarters on Sydam Street (twice), on Hart Street and eventually in 1932 (until 1940) at 295 Stanhope Street.

The reason for the moves was obvious. The family grew and its needs changed, as did Avedis' earning capacity. All the moves were no more than one mile from each other, and all were confined to the area in Brooklyn known as Brooklyn-Ridgewood. Some of the apartments had no central heating. They were known as "cold water flats." A pot-bellied stove was our only means of warmth. Lower

Ridgewood was a bustling Italian neighborhood. It was loud, raucous, and always alive. The streets were open fairgrounds, and the smells and sounds of the ethnic Sicilians permeated every apartment. There were few (if any) private homes, with three, four and five story buildings offering the "railroad" apartments at twenty or thirty dollars rent per month. Candy stores, fruit and deli markets (with most of their wares displayed outside the buildings) and small movie houses made up the flavor of the neighborhood. Pushcarts, ice wagons and other mobile (horse drawn or hand pushed) vehicles flowed with predictable regularity through the crowded streets. The smells of garlic and wine, of cheese and bacula (smoked, dried codfish), of tobacco and of outside garbage cans are still infused in my childhood memories.

There were few cars, so children played freely in the streets. They played the unique games of New York City with vigor and gusto as their mothers often watched from apartment windows. Fathers such as Avedis worked long and hard hours, but somehow always returned home with a smile. While working at Brooklyn Better Bleach, Avedis awoke at 5:00AM and took public transportation to work. His work early on, as an inexperienced furrier, required him to clean the pelt of the furs. A laborious task called "scraping." Later he would dye and grade pelts. Most evenings Avedis would not return until

7:00PM. I cannot recall if he worked Saturdays, but most jobs were six days a week.

My memories of the eight years our family of five lived at 295 Stanhope Street are vivid. Those were the days that led to unemployment, scarcity, and even hunger. I remember little of that. Our enclave was always secure. Our happiness and security were never threatened. Thanks to our parents we passed through the depression years with few scars, and much appreciation for the gift of sharing.

In the summer of 1940 we left the apartment in lower Ridgewood where we had lived for the greatest number of years (eight). Again it was Pop, who had returned to his job as a furrier, and whose salary was now stable, who took us from Brooklyn to Ridgewood, Queens. Actually our new home in upper Ridgewood was but one block across the border from Brooklyn. But the difference of the fifteen blocks or so between 295 Stanhope Street and 1740 Menahan Street were significant and sharply distinct. This new neighborhood was culturally "old" German. For New York City, it was conservative, unusually quiet, and spotlessly clean. A stark difference from the energy of Brooklyn-Ridgewood. Most of the houses were smaller, two or three stories high. The apartments however were larger, five or six rooms, and were more modem. Steam-heat was the norm but the age of air conditioning was still 25 years away - except for the movie theaters.

The streets were seldom strewn with any litter. Curbsides were tree-lined and avenues almost park-like. The women would meticulously scrub the stairs (called stoops) of their buildings each Saturday morning with hot sudsy water. The act was almost a religious ritual. Good conduct and respect were neighborhood traits. Any boisterous act would be reprimanded and the parents of unruly children would be advised to control their offspring.

Old country German self-control was the prevailing attitude. Perhaps this cultural shock was compounded by the depression. In any case, upper Ridgewood was a fine, safe, cultivated neighborhood in which to grow up.

It was from this third floor, six-room apartment on Menahan Street that many of my childhood memories were born. We lived here for nineteen years. Avedis became secure in his job here, although he continued to work long, hard hours. Dick and Mary completed their high school education while living here. Dick continued his schooling taking night classes at St. Johns, Fordham and the New School, while working full time at Mr. Sahagian's plant, "Pictorial Photoengraving Company." Mary got her first job at the Catholic Book Publishing Company. It was while living here that Pearl Harbor interrupted all our lives. World War II was an epic time for all Americans.

Dick and cousin Souren ("Sam") Dermengian joined the fight almost immediately. Dick served in the Air Corps, and in Intelligence. He was stationed in Africa and South America. Sam saw action in Europe and was wounded by enemy fire during the "Battle of the Bulge."

Avedis and Ardemis suffered through the days of the war. They both worried intensely about Dick. Both had already lost so many in their respective families. They still grieved the loss of their baby son Souren. Any further loss would be unbearable. Avedis experienced his first heart attack in 1942. He was 52 years old. Avedis had seen enough of heartbreaks and death. How he wanted Dick home and the war to end. Dick returned safely home in 1945, and we celebrated the safe return of all our boys as the war ended.

It was at this time that Pop suffered a second heart attack, and was, in time, convinced by Ardemis to retire. The commute to New Jersey was becoming too difficult. Avedis left work with great reluctance. He was always the family leader, the breadwinner, and always a worker.

Eldest son Dick, newly returned from the war, purchased his first car, a 1939 Nash, with his army separation pay. It was stolen the very first night he owned it. Ardemis looked out of the window early at first light to admire the Sarajians' first car and it was gone! She woke Dick and he ran downstairs and into the street (in his underwear I think) to check it out. The car was recovered months later in Philadelphia.

We greeted the post-war years with incredible excitement, enthusiasm and hope. It was an age of confidence and boundless optimism. We were all together, reborn, with the dark days of genocide, depression and two world wars far behind us.

B. Ardemis' Siblings: World War II and Post-War

Kaloust, who attended night school to improve his English, became so proficient that he spoke America's native tongue with nary an accent. Kaloust was among only a handful of exiled Armenians who conversed, wrote, and read perfect "American" English. He had become a fully integrated Armenian-American. Kaloust continued to live with Aghavni and Mirijan for a short period of time before he moved to Brooklyn and lived with Avedis and Ardemis.

In 1925, Kaloust found his true love, Keghanoush Agababian. Keghanoush, a wonderful and beautiful girl, was an immigrant from a small village outside of Erzurum, called Papert. She radiated joy and happiness, and she quickly captured Kaloust's heart. In 1926 they were wed in New York City. Shortly thereafter, they had their first-born Keghvart ("Kay"). Kaloust was the last of the Sergenian clan to marry and the last to have children. He and his family moved to Boston, where Keghanoush blessed Kaloust with three more beautiful daughters, Araxie, Anahid and Sona.

114

All four girls were fair skinned, attractive and gifted. Each girl had her own distinctive style and charm. The one trait that Keghanoush and Kaloust instilled in Kay, Araxy, Anahid and Sona was a thirst for knowledge. The girls were all college educated at a time when most females did not even think attending university. I believe Kay was the first of all the "Sergenian offspring" to earn a college degree. Along with their formal education, the girls were schooled in the cultural disciplines. Piano and violin lessons were a part of their daily routine, along with dance and ballet lessons.

Keghanoush, a marvelous cook and homemaker, also imbued the art of Armenian cuisine into her daughters. Never to be forgotten were lessons in the Armenian language along with the history of their heritage. Perhaps the only gap in their education was the single common omission that most Armenian parents imposed upon their young. The horrors of the Genocide were spoken only in whispers and in gossamer thin tales, never to be explained or explored. The hearts and minds of the young were considered too sensitive and fragile to be defiled with the terror, which their parents desperately tried to suppress in their own consciousness.

The girls all grew into wonderful adults. They married and blessed Kaloust and Keghanoush with eleven grandchildren. Five of these grandchildren were boys. None of the Sergenian men, Andon or

Kaloust, fathered a son. So, although the genes live on, the Sergenian name which was passed along from the union of Sarkis to Anna, in the wild mountains of Shabin Karahisar, found its' end in the hallowed and peaceful grave sites of America.

Kaloust and Keghanoush became fully integrated into the lifestyle of America. Keghanoush even learned to drive a car and gained her license (and independence). Kaloust became the top salesman and chief buyer of oriental rugs for one of Boston's largest department stores, Paine Furniture. He died in 1983 and Keghanoush, his devoted spouse, survived him until 1995. She was ninety years old at the time of her death.

The memories of times shared with Uncle Kaloust and Morak (Aunty Keghanoush) and the girls were especially precious to our family. Love and affection between the families endured and even deepened through the years. We will always cherish and celebrate their lives as truly remarkable people. They were heroic Armenians and our pioneers in America. The handsomely elegant, intellectual, warm, loving and caring Kaloust was a role model, not only for our family, but also for all who knew him.

I lovingly recall Uncle Kaloust as a ruggedly handsome, warm, generous man. He was deeply emotional, caring and giving. He encouraged us to be the best we could be academically. He was deeply religious and worked fervently for his church, his nation, and his family. He always signed his letters to me during my tour in the U.S. Army with "Your Devoted Uncle." And this is what he was, devoted to all of us, and us to him. He was our "Dai-Dai", and our love for him was boundless.

As for Aghavni and Mirijan, Aghavni gave birth to the first of their two children, Souren ("Sam") in 1922. Sam was named in memory of Aghavni's lost brother and after a son of Mirijan's slain during the Genocide. In 1925, Aghavni gave birth to Arouse. Mirijan again took the occasion to name his newborn daughter after another of his six martyred children. The Dermengians moved uptown to the Washington Heights section of Manhattan, and later to the Bronx. I believe they were the first of the Sergenians to own their own home.

Mirijan worked hard in his trade selling oriental carpets. He was among the first of the American-Armenians to own a car, and drove it gallantly if not defiantly without a driver's license. As a youth and as an adult Mirijan remained a joyful, spirited, fun-loving man. He was always gentle, generous and selfless to all his family and friends. I still recall his rich tenor voice as he joyfully sang Armenian folk songs at our family gatherings. His talents were passed on to his immensely gifted son, Sam, and to his lovely and talented daughter Arouse.

Arouse's wonderful son, Paul, lived with his mother in Southern California until her death in 2008. Paul, himself a valiant survivor, has faced the physical disabilities of cerebral palsy. But his determination, his intellect, his will and his soaring spirit have elevated Paul above his infirmities. Paul's sister Ani is still another sparkling gem, and inheritor of the "Sergenian spirit."

The Dermengians left New York City in the late 1940s for the sunshine of California. Our irrepressible Morak Aghavni had made another of her unshakable and formidable decisions. Her daughter Arouse was now ready for the glitter of the American Silver Screen. Arouse, (sometimes called "Rose") was gifted with a full, rich and vibrant voice. She had attained local fame by singing in the chorus of the New York Metropolitan Opera, and had recorded her voice on a number of records. Arouse, however talented and beautiful, did not have the relentless drive of her mother, and movies were not to be. Arouse eventually married and settled in Los Angles. "Morkurar" Mirijan and "Morak" Aghavni lived the last few years of their lives in a senior residence just outside Los Angeles. They were totally devoted to each other, to their son and daughter, and to their four grandchildren. Mirijan died in 1972 at the age of ninety-one. Aghavni lived for two more years, until 1974. She died at age seventy-eight.

Chapter 18

Avedis and Ardemis' Family Grows

Dick courted Arax Catchouny and in May of 1950 they were wed. In March 1951, I enlisted in the Army during the Korean War, and returned safely three years later. In 1954 Avedis, Ardemis, Mary and Haig bought their first "family" car, a 1954 Ford Fairlane.

With the birth of Dick and Arax's three children, Avedis and Ardemis became grandparents, and a light shone in their eyes as never before. Mary became an aunt and Haig an uncle and Godfather. Those happy years brought us Rich in 1951, Ken in 1953 and Carol in 1957. Although Avedis suffered some severe health issues in his 60's and 70's, he immensely enjoyed his growing family. Holidays, birthdays, and anniversaries were his favorite times.

Nothing pleased him more than preparing his Armenian delicacies during our festive celebrations. He loved to cook and bake, and directed "his assistant Ardemis" as would a master chef instructing an apprentice. He never lost the flair he had acquired as a restaurant chef. Avedis enjoyed cooking at all times. He planned Sunday dinners well in advance. Of course Ardemis did the bulk of the everyday cooking. The specialties, however, were "John's" domain. Whether it was "basturma and eggs" on Saturday morning, or Sou Boreg or Monte for Sunday lunch, Avedis always had something special to share.

As the 1950's drew to a close, another chapter in Avedis Sarajian's life was to end. The owner of our apartment building at 1740 Menahan Street, a widow, Mrs. Pfiefer, died of old age. Her son Ted, who had recently married, wanted to return to his old home. Since Mrs. Pfiefer had shared the owner's apartment on the first floor with another elderly couple, it was not available.

We were asked, nicely I suppose, to find another home. Avedis, now 69 years old, promptly found a ground floor apartment in a two-family house, a few doors away from his friend and fellow Efkeretsi, Baron Mardiros Touvalian. The new apartment was more modern than the old one. It was convenient to the subway and bus for commuting, and a Bohack Super Market was located on the corner. Of course, the move from 1740 was sad, nostalgic, and tears were shed, but Avedis again found a way to upgrade his family's living conditions. The move was just six or seven blocks, but it served to give a lift to all of us. Avedis now content with his retirement, spent time with his friends Baron Mardiros and Baron Hagop. He made new friends as well, one being the father of the notorious Mafia kingpin and godfather Joe Bonano.

Avedis would spend warm days sitting outside the apartment in a lawn chair, reading his "Hairenik" and greeting friends and neighbors. I believe he felt quite content. As always he had his "Ardem" to comfort him, and his daughter and son at home as well. It was from here, 1744 De Kalb Avenue, where Avedis was struck with stomach cancer. Fortunately, the disease was diagnosed early, and after radical stomach surgery, Avedis made a full recovery.

Soon after his return to health, Avedis and Ardemis helped celebrate the wedding of Haig to Mary Kachian in September 1962. Things were on the upswing again. Avedis' boys were now settled, and they had even become partners with Avedis' old friend, Baron Edward Sahagian in Pictorial Photo Engraving Company.

Haig and Mary also bought a house in New Jersey, near Dick and Arax. Avedis had two sons who owned their own homes and he was proud. He himself always wanted a private house. Ardemis was too cautious and careful with family funds to sanction such a financial risk.

In August of 1965, Mary and Haig had a daughter, Nadine, to add more joy to the Sarajian household. In October 1966, Michael came along (bearing a remarkable resemblance to Avedis). This completed the blessed package of five grandchildren for Avedis and Ardemis. The aging couple drew no greater happiness than sharing time and loving all their grandchildren. What a gift! From the hills of Efkere and the mountains of Karahisar to the sanctuary of America; the Sarajian-Sergenian legacy had been written.

A few months after Avedis held his last grandson Michael in his arms, he was called to his Lord. At home, with his wife and daughter beside him, Avedis died of a heart attack on Armenian Christmas day, January 6, 1967. He was 76 years old. Dick and Haig hurried to his side in the early morning hours, but were unable to share their father's last moments. There was always more to say to each other. To tell him of their love, and thank him for his sacrifices. He was a model and inspiration. He left an indelible mark of goodness on Ardemis, Dikran, Mary and Haig.

Chapter 19

Ardemis without Avedis

When Avedis died in 1967, Ardemis was sixty-five years old. Their age difference of twelve years never mattered much to them, but now, Ardemis had many years left to her, without the strong hand of her husband to share her life.

My sister Mary had been the breadwinner for the family after Avedis' retirement. She continued in that role after he died and provided constant support, both financial and emotional, to Ardemis. Mary and Mom lived together, first in a Teaneck, New Jersey apartment, and later in Hackensack, New Jersey. Their life together was warm and devoted, and they enjoyed all the family festivities of the holidays and birthdays with Dick and Haig and their families. For twenty-five years Ardemis received the daily loving

123

care of her daughter. Mary, in turn, received the tender adoration of her mother.

During the last few months of 1991, Ardemis' health was beginning to wane. Her spark was dimming and her time here, with us, was nearing its end. During our Christmas Eve celebration at Dick and Arax's home in 1991, Ardemis was too weak to attend. Her children took turns staying with her in her apartment, where she slept peacefully.

One week later, on January 2nd, she failed to respond to Mary and was taken to Holy Name Hospital in Teaneck by ambulance. Mary called her two brothers to be with her, and we prayed for our mother's recovery. In mid-afternoon, while Ardemis seemed to be sleeping comfortably, Dick, Mary and I took a lunch break for about one hour.

When we returned, (I was first into her hospital room), we noticed she no longer had the oxygen tubes at her nostrils. I remarked that she must have been recovering. As I bent to kiss her, the nurse rushed into the room, and told us that Ardemis had died while we were away. My dear mother could not even bear to sadden her children with her moment of departure. We held each other and cried.

A few moments later a nun came into the room and offered solace, and we prayed together. Dick called our "Hayr Soorp" (Priest), and Hayr Soorp Nareg came quickly and stayed with us for the rest of the day and night. We all returned to tell our wives and children of our loss. Hayr Soorp Nareg was with us as we comforted each other in our grief.

After notifying friends and family we made all the necessary arrangements. Dick, Mary and I, our wives and children, received our loved ones and shared our loss, and recalled our joys. Even today I can remember spending hours next to Mom at her casket, astonished how beautiful she still looked. I wanted to ingrain her earthly features into my memory, never to forget. Really, it was unnecessary; for how could I ever forget?

Hayr Nareg spoke eloquently at the service in the funeral home. The following day, a clear and very cold January morn, the funeral service was held at our church, Sts. Vartanantz. Our Prelate, Archbishop Mesrop Ashjian eulogized Ardemis' time and passage with us. I think Ardemis might have been a bit embarrassed by "Surpazan's" impassioned remembrances. We all wept at his words, and then journeyed to Cedar Grove Cemetery where her body was put to rest with Avedis and their spirits soared, at last free and reunited.

We, the inheritors of their sacrifices, will never forget the terrible hardships they endured so that we could live in freedom here in America. Part of their story has been written, but the responsibilities they accepted years ago, and the impact of their deeds, will live on in the generations they saved. They were, Andon and Shushan, Aghavni and Mirijan,

Kaloust and Keghanoush, and Ardemis and Avedis.
We remember them in joy and with happy heart.

Chapter 20

Remembrances of My Parents

It is difficult to recapture a lifetime of memories and retell them on a few pages. When trying to convey the essence of your parents, sharing all that he or she was, is virtually impossible. For the children of parents who had escaped the horrors of Genocide this task is even more difficult. My parents were essentially who they were because of the history that they had overcome. Their essence or being was created out of hardship. Their role as parents was affected as well.

Both of my parents were fiercely devoted to family because they knew what it was like to have your family taken from you at a moment's notice. The efforts of both Ardemis and Avedis were directed to enhance and support our family. Their personal pleasures and I knew of only a few, stood far behind their overwhelming love of family.

My father was profoundly protective of his brood and worked tirelessly to provide on their behalf. Although he enjoyed showing a stern side, he was in fact an extremely gentle, sentimental and sensitive soul. He wept easily and unashamedly. His weakness was his passionate demeanor. He would express himself openly and with fervor. However, he was also careful to be in control, and conducted himself with grace and dignity.

You would never find Avedis unkempt in any sense. He never allowed himself to be seen unshaven, or without his dentures. He was meticulously clean, even though his hands bore the marks of his hard labors; Avedis enjoyed being dressed in style. He almost always wore a hat when outdoors and seldom dressed casually.

Watching Avedis eat gave you a clue to his careful social conduct. He ate moderate sized and well-balanced meals, never in excess. He cut his food precisely, and ate and drank without haste. Avedis seldom used alcohol, but as his generation was want to do; he did enjoy tobacco until his heart attacks eliminated that pleasure.

Avedis freely exhibited his affection for his loved ones. He would hug and kiss at every opportunity. For his immediate family, his kisses sometimes had a "bite" attached to them. Kind of playful family "branding" or "hickey." His inclination to be openly expressive with family and friends has been passed along to his children.

Although his health suffered in his last twenty-five years, Avedis never complained. His loving wife "Ardem" was always at his side to care and comfort him. Their devotion to each other would be a benchmark on how to be married. They were the perfect complement to each other. Avedis was expressive and expansive. He was sentimental and wore his feelings on his sleeve for all to see. Ardemis' nature was introverted and introspective, carefully sheltering her emotions. She was suspicious of anything that could be a threat to her family. They were both sensitive, but he outwardly and she inwardly.

Avedis and Ardemis argued openly with enthusiasm, but never with malice. Their love for each other would not permit otherwise. They had suffered great inhumanities, and their strength for the remainder of their lives was dependent upon their union.

The nametag on our doorbell read A. Sarajian. It was not Avedis or Ardemis but simply "A" as if they had merged, two separate but one. Both of my parents were eternally grateful for their good fortune of being Americans and were proud to be American citizens. Of course they never relinquished their ties to their roots. To their cores they were both Armenians. They believed that in order to be a good Americans, they needed to first be good Armenians.

Avedis particularly embraced his Armenian Church with his heart and soul. The devastations, which occurred early in his life, did not drive "Asdavatz" (God) from his being. His beliefs in God helped comfort his grief. Politically he was a supportive "Dashnag," and a Roosevelt Democrat. As a young man Avedis was active in both church service (Board of Trustees of St. Illuminator's) and in local government politics. Avedis found little time later in his life for such activities. His determination and resolve to provide all he could for his family was his adult compulsion. Avedis did, however, maintain his close relationship with his Efkeretsi brotherhood through most of his adult years. Besides sharing friendships, the "Miatuin" ("Society") Club collected and solicited funds for a girls' school in Efkere before the Genocide. After the massacres, the Efkeretsi brotherhood worked diligently to acquire relief funds to aid the refugees in America. Avedis, for a time, was president of the New York chapter of the Efkeretsi Miatuin.

Both of my parents appeared to me to be so gentle, but they sustained an inner force of ethics and strength. I always felt safe in their presence. Avedis laughed heartily, and cried somberly. Both parents were always open with us, but could never find the means to share their past with us. I think that Dick, Mary and I felt we were deprived of the knowledge of their "other life." For Avedis, this was his dark secret. For all the years I knew him he stubbornly confined these painful secrets of his early life to a shrouded comer of his mind, always apart from us. Never did he disclose any of the facts of his family in Turkey to us. I suppose that its revelation would carry too high a cost for Avedis to bear. Ardemis held on to these secrets until she was nearing the end of her life; at that time determined to share the truth with her kin.

Avedis loved, with boundless passion, his America and his Armenia, and despised its' foes. He yearned for justice, and rejoiced at America's victories in war, and hungered for the world's indictment of the Turks for the massacres and genocide against his people. His wounds from 1915, as for all Armenians, remained open and festering.

For us, his children, Avedis worked exhaustively. His labors never seemed to cease, but he never asked us to share his burden. He was generous and resourceful. He was modest and unassuming. But he also was fiercely proud and stubborn. He wanted little for himself, but nothing but the best for his family, his country and his people. If he had shortcomings, I suppose he gave too much of himself for us. He had few other pleasures in life.

In January of 1967, after the funeral services for our father, the traditional memorial dinner was held at a local Armenian restaurant. Mr. Edward Sahagian delivered the eulogy. Baron Edward depicted Avedis as a "simple" man. I found myself upset and disappointed at this characterization.

Something with more depth and meaning, expressed in glowing terms, which exalted the life, and works of Avedis Sarajian is what I expected.

Baron Sahagian, after all, was among the erudite orators of the Armenian community. He was lucid and polished, and spoke with remarkable ease in both English and Armenian. He was, additionally, an extremely close and dear friend to my father.

Now, after many years, I realized that "simple" as used by Mr. Sahagian was not a demeaning, insulting description of his friend. Rather, its use fit our father quite well. Avedis was simple. He was uncomplicated and basically unadorned. His life was convoluted with twists and turns, complicated with the fortunes and misfortunes of fate. He had endured a turbulent early life, stained with heart-wrenching periods of terrible strife. Later, he glowed in life's pleasures of love, happiness, and joy of family. His focus, his ethics, his manners were "straight on." His disappointments and devastations did not alter the honest course of his life. Yes, after all was said and done, he remained, and was simple. Simply Wonderful.

Even on his grave, which he shares with his beloved "Ardem," stands a granite stone, not unlike the stones of Efkere. The inscription simply reads "Avedis Sarajian, beloved husband and father, born in Efkere, October 16, 1890, died January 6, 1967." A small simple stone with a simple inscription. But to all of us whom he touched he was mighty, a giant!

Looking back on my time with Ardemis, I know I discovered, or uncovered some of her "secret tales" but sadly, never before did I appreciate the profundity of what she, her siblings and her generation accomplished. I don't believe that they themselves realized what odds were conquered. Somewhere in these writings I make reference to Ardemis' "Guardian Angel." Truly I believe that these four "Sergenians" were protected for a reason that only God knows.

Chapter 21

The Next Generation: Dick and Mary

A. My Brother Dick

When I was born, Avedis was already forty years old. Ardemis was twenty-eight. Dick had just passed his eighth birthday and Mary was six. From early on, through my childhood and into my teens, I looked to my older, wiser brother as a guide, a model to ease my own tenuous passage into the grown-up world of first generation America. I often felt uneasy with a sense "that my parents were kind of foreigners" in our American environment. Mary and Dick weren't too bad. Dick especially fit the perfect mold for me. If only I could copy him?

From the very beginning Dick was caring, giving, helpful and never a mean or bossy big brother. He would talk, help and explain things to

134

me. He was understanding and his approach was easy, casual, and natural. Mary was a girl and Mom and Pop were, you know, Mom and Pop: the law! Dick knew things, showed me things. He looked like I wanted to look, walked and talked that way too. But I was never jealous. Dick's goodness would not allow that. Dick gave freely in such a way that anyone, neither you nor I, would ever feel obligated, constrained or pressured to return his kindness or favor.

Come to think of it, I don't believe Dick derived any satisfaction for his good deeds. I don't think he ever considered his benevolence as being anything but natural everyday occurrence.

In the October - November 2006 issue of "Outreach," our church publication, the initial article was a multi-columned biography of Dick's service to the Church. The warmth expressed in this heart-tugging, tear wiping editorial was authored by one our dearest friends and certainly a kindred spirit of my brother, Iris Papazian. The article was entitled, "Dick Sarajian – What can I do for you?" That was a question commonplace in any opening conversation you had with Dick. Iris wrote with sensitivity and affection of Dick's unfailing responsiveness and willingness to be of service. No matter how difficult the project, no matter how unrewarding the cause, Dick's humble manner, his generous and unpretentious temperament and his legendary work ethic accepted every challenge with enthusiasm and a smile.

Dick was honored by many, in correspondence, by testimonials, awards, plaques, medals and decorations. Among those who paid tribute to Dick were four generations in the hierarchy of our Armenian clergy. Dick was cited by four Catholicoi and five Prelates of our Church. If you knew Dick you also knew that he never wore his honors on his chest or sleeve. Instead, he kept them tucked safely away in a corner of his soul, somewhat uncomfortable that his embarrassment might show. Dick exhibited so many facets of goodness he was difficult to describe in a word or phrase. The one word most attributed to my brother was "beloved." I guess those seven letters say it all.

During the past months since his passing, I have often dwelled on the lifetime of memories we shared. These recollections were reinforced during my many personal and intimate visits with him during the past ten years. We would reminisce, often laugh, sometimes cry and even occasionally sing. His wife Arax and children mentioned that I cheered him during his uncomplaining years of infirmity. I'm not sure if they realize how much I drew from him.

I know it may be self indulgent but I would very much like to share some of these loving moments within the following pages of script. I know it will help me to complete my own portrait of the most influential and unforgettable man in my life.

I'll try to guide you down the lane chronologically, but I may skip a beat or two. If I do, speak with anyone who knew Dick. We all marched a happy step to his beat.

My earliest thoughts of Dick, like in an old movie, are in shades of black and white. The opening scenes are hued in gloom and despair, but the happy ending closes with the white sparkle of joy and relief. The year must be 1935 or 1936 and Dick was a weak, very, very sick early teenager. He was struck down with rheumatic fever, many times a fatal disease. Avedis and Ardemis were near hysteria as Dick was taken away on stretcher to Wyckoff Heights Hospital, just a few blocks away. Eight years earlier the agonizing Armenian couple had lost their infant son, Souren, at the same hospital.

My next flickering flashback is of Dick coming home, weak and wane, but thank God, recovering. His hospital confinement must have been weeks, if not months. At home, the window shades were up and sunlight streamed in. Strangely, when Dick stood up he looked so much taller that I remembered and, almost grown up, a young man. Another flash memory I remember, the whole house was aglow, sparkling. I think it was spring, sweet spring. Everything smelled better, looked better tasted better, felt better. Dick was home!

After a few years down the line I recall being in bed myself, ill with the childhood disease of mumps. To the family's chagrin, I infected Dick.

We must have been sharing the same bedroom for I remember him there, with me. Much later, I learned that mumps, contracted by an adult, could lead to infertility. Thank goodness the unborn lives of Rich, Ken and Carol were not compromised.

On the lighter side, Dick and I would reminisce about our childhood, the pillow fights we enjoyed on weekend mornings. Dick always let me win. Who could forget the stacks of comic books, tied with string, he would lug home from the house of his best buddy Hubie Lazzeri. Mary and I indulged ourselves in the fantasies of Superman, Batman, The Torch, Captain Marvel and the Submariner. At one time I reminded Dick that he gave me my first two hard covered books, Last of the Mohicans and Arabian Nights. Dick encouraged me to read, and helped me get my first library card. He opened new worlds for me and sparked my imagination into new frontiers. Dick's guidance of me was invaluable, not only for me, but for yet an unborn generation. I think Dick honed his nurturing skills so well on me that years later his own children benefited and they all turned out great.

During the 1930's there took place a few incidents regarding Dick of which I have no personal recall. Rather, each of the following amusing stories fall into the category of "family folk tales." And each episode will buff a brighter glow into the shining star that was Dick.

When I was five or six years old I was, for some long forgotten reason, left in the care of Dick for a full day. We were alone at home and if my math is correct Dick was almost fourteen years old and certainly responsible for his age. The story goes that it was a Saturday afternoon and there was a film playing at the local movie house that Dick longed to see. The theater was only a few blocks from our apartment in Ridgewood, Brooklyn. I'm not sure if Dick had an O.K from our parents, (I doubt it) but he took me to the movie. I believe the cost of a Saturday matinee was five cents and probably two pennies for me. During the movie Dick needed to use the rest room. He made me promise not to leave my seat. Back in the 30's movie houses hired mature women who would act as matrons. Their primary responsibility was to maintain order among the younger set. Each matron was armed with a flashlight. Well, it seems a bright beam frightened me and I bolted out of the movie house. When Dick returned to his seat he was mortified that his little brother had disappeared. Dick frantically ran out of the theatre and began searching the streets. Adjacent to the theatre, (it was either the "Starr" or "Willoughby" theater), there was a neighborhood park and playground. Somehow, I had found my way there, wandering about aimlessly. Fortunately for me, in short order Dick discovered me. Here my brother's true nature came forth. He never questioned my "flight from fright." He never admonished me with "How could you?" or "You promised," or "What's wrong with you." He was so happy I was safe he only held, comforted and kissed me. I must have been scared, and in tears. Dick's concern was not of his "loss," but of my plight. Dick was just fourteen years old, but he was pure fourteen carats, genuine and untarnished, our golden boy.

A year or two later that very same park was the setting for another family tale. During the days of the depression every youngster wanted to contribute to the family income. I had "whined" to my mother that I wanted to sell pretzels in the park "to make some money." Finally Mom relented. She fashioned a "pretzel basket" for me from a small oval egg crate (common at that time). She placed a clean, fresh dishtowel into the basket and took me by the hand to the "pretzel factory." This establishment was located in the basement of our local bakery. Early in the morning vendors would line up to purchase the newly baked, hot, salted pretzels for the remarkable price of two for a penny. The selling price was a penny each. Some years later we would see "jumbo" pretzels selling for three cents. Mom put down a dime and we left with twenty of the hot, tasty, Brooklyn delicacies. I carefully covered my wares with the dish towel to "insure freshness." Mom walked me to the park and playground and left me to my own devices (those were trusting times). Mom then went to a nearby store to shop. As I scanned the play area looking for prospective buyers, I spotted Dick and sister Mary with some of their friends. It wasn't long before all my pretzels were gone. When Mom returned and found me "pretzel less" she asked for an accounting. Looking downcast, I admitted to having no money, no profits and no cash. I was penniless. Mom asked what happened. Big-hearted Dick had convinced both me and our sister (Mary would always, always listen to Dick), that we should "play nice" and share our yummy morsels with all the kids on the block. I'm sure Mom and Pop had a few choice words regarding and emphasizing the "conservation of family funds" to both Dick and Mary. The point of this parable is that my wondrous brother did have faults. His heart was always bigger that his pocketbook.

To close this 1930's trilogy I will retell a story that happened later in the decade. My father chose to live in Ridgewood because he had a clique of "Efkeretsis" that lived nearby. Avedis and his countrymen were close friends and saw each other frequently. Most of the men were married and were deeply absorbed in raising their young families. One young boy, Jackie, the son of Pop's dear friend Paroog Sinamian, had been taken critically ill and was rushed to our neighborhood hospital, Wyckoff Heights. The teenager had experienced a ruptured or as we called it a "burst appendix." He was now suffering from blood poisoning. Dick had overheard Mr. Sinamian tearfully telling his compatriots of his son's grave condition. The boy, Jackie, was in dire need of a blood transfusion as he lay near death in a hospital ward. Unhesitatingly, asking no one, Dick ran (not walked) to the hospital and offered his blood in an effort to save Jack's life. I'm not sure if medical science even knew much about blood-matching, but I heard that Dick was hooked up, arm to arm, vein to vein, in a desperate effort to pump fresh, clean blood into Jackie. Dick's valiant effort did not save Jackie's life, but his selfless action, his heart and desire to aid became a part of the legend that defined my brother.

Recently, I have had a correspondence with Jackie's youngest sister Kathleen in California. She wrote to me offering condolences after hearing of Dick's death from an older sister, Mary. Kathy is a few years younger than I am, so she has little personal memory of the tragedy. However, in her letter she confirms how the story of Dick's rush to help is told and retold. Dick's efforts were not forgotten, but remain alive in Sinamian family lore. If you search about, Dick has touched many as he touched the Sinamians.

When Dick joined the Army Air Corps at the very onset of World War Two, I was the proudest kid on the block. I remember rushing out and buying the window pennant with the blue star in the center. It signified that a member of the family was in the armed forces. A gold star, and no one wanted one, meant a serviceman had lost his life.

One day in the fall of 1942 Dick and cousin Souren were both home on leave. Without warning the two G.I.'s escorted me to Grover Cleveland High School, and into the gym area where they enrolled me into Troop 131 of the Boy Scouts. Later, Dick bought me my first Scout uniform. He asked Mom to hide it beneath her bed, until Christmas, when I was presented with my own <u>uniform</u>. (Men in uniform was a big thing for me in 1942.)

Oh yes, I almost forgot, years earlier Dick also took me to P.S. 81 to enroll me as a new student. Dick met with and introduced me to the Principal, Mr. Vlyman. Our family had moved from Stanhope Street to Menahan Street (about half a mile), and Dick was delegated to make sure I got off to a good start at my new school. Mr. Vlyman, a serious, austere man, spoke at some length with Dick. Before we left the school the Principal put his hand on my shoulder, leaned down and whispered, "A fine brother you have son." That's a phrase I have heard countless times. And it gave me goose bumps every time!

In 1942 Dick inadvertently opened another door for me to enter. Sister Mary and I were writing weekly letters to Dick during the four years he served in the military. I recall we wrote on a single thin sheeted (onion-skin) piece of paper which folded to become its own envelope. The format was called "V" Mail. Hence my communicating skills were first honed and developed years ago as I kept in touch with my big brother. A decade later the roles were reversed and Dick and Mary kept my spirits up with weekly mail from the home front. In the span of those seven years (four for Dick's service and three for mine) I never again wrote or received as many letters and I'm sure the same could be said for my brother and sister. In 1945 Dick came home from the war. He had volunteered almost immediately after Pearl Harbor and took his place with honor and distinction among those whom we now call "the Greatest Generation." Dick was fortunate he bore no battle scars from combat. He was however, now four years older and wearied and weakened by frequent bouts of malaria. He also battled occasional episodes of dysentery. But he was whole and he was home!

At the precise moment of Dick's return I was the one who had answered his ring of the doorbell. The family occupied the third floor apartment at 1740 Menahan Street in Ridgewood, Queens. When I realized it was Dick I flew down the three flights at an amazing pace, (my fastest ever) and embraced Dick. I was the first to say "Welcome Home."

Dick returned to his old job at Pictorial Engraving and was rewarded with an apprenticeship. He also continued his education during the evening hours. He attended (at different times of course) Fordham University, St. John's and the New School of Social Research.

At home during the next few years Dick suffered from recurrent attacks of malaria. It must have taken fifteen years or more before his immune system defeated the "bug." It was Mom, and Doctors Cook and Grober who helped Dick at home, and his life's mate Arax who nursed him after they were married.

Once settled at home, Dick became active and a leader in the Armenian Youth Federation. He offered his support and guidance to me if I was "interested in joining" but he never insisted or pushed for my compliance. Of course I was always too engrossed in my own teenage world. School, sports, scouting and a neighborhood social club took up most of my time. In the late 1940's Dick encouraged me to pursue the study and playing of a musical instrument. He even offered to pay for lessons. Dick almost had me convinced with intriguing stories of a strange stringed instrument he called an OUD. But again I said "no thanks" I wanted no part of the ethnic Armenian world that now surrounded and enthralled my brother. Again, Dick never insisted. He only opened doors and invited me in. I was more into playing stickball or softball, using the very same baseball glove (my first) Dick had sent to me from Africa in 1944.

Sometime in early 1946, Mom, Pop and Dick discussed my future, but without me in attendance. Pop had used his influence with his Efkeretsi friend, Mr. Edward Sahagian, to get Dick into his Photoengraving shop and eventually to gain an apprenticeship. Now it was my turn to be introduced into the world of ink and paper, of copper and zinc, of magnesium chalk and "dragon's blood." Dick arranged to get me a summer job as an errand boy during the summers of 1946 and 1947. This would be my first work experience, outside of selling pretzels back in 1936, or delivering morning newspapers during the early 1940's. My entry into Pictorial Engraving also launched my career into an industry in which I would be employed during the next fifty-two years. This one act provided me with the financial means to eventually marry and raise a family.

After starting my job as a messenger Dick and I initiated a ritual which had its earliest roots in my father's affectionate nature. Avedis punctuated every greeting and departure with family and close friends with a kiss. Dick and I naturally fell into the routine and it became an "iron-bound ritual" for a lifetime, even in our work place. I'm sure, through the years, many onlookers would question these two brothers who always seemed to be kissing, but to us it was as instinctive as shaking hands or a wave goodbye or hello.

And speaking of shaking hands, while Dick and cousin Souren were still teenagers they somehow developed a secret handshake. I don't believe it ever had any mysterious ritualistic significance. The "shake" consisted of four moves repeated three times, in accelerating succession and ended with a flourishing break leaving the thumb up, fist closed in the classic hitch-hiker pose. Again, I have no knowledge of its origin, but the "digi-axiom" has been passed along to all family youngsters as the "Sarajian Shake".

The greeting and departing family kiss, the frequent hugs and tousling of hair and even the inconsequential handshake are all symptoms of my family's warm demeanor. I will always be grateful for my exposure into this infectious bacterium of unquestioned affection. I believe it to be a condition that is virulent in most Armenians.

In the late 40's, I was struggling with the difficult curriculum at my scholarship high school of Brooklyn Tech. Dick was always there to encourage me in ways that were not so easy or familiar to my mother or father.

In 1950 I stood as "Best Man" for Dick and Arax, but we all know who the "best man" was, is, and will always be!

In 1951 with a war raging in Korea, Dick advised me to enlist into the military rather than wait and be drafted. This time I heeded his council and so discovered a branch in the Army called the Army Security Agency. Among their varied activities with which the ASA was involved with was code breaking – cryptography. Perfect, since Dick did this work during World War II, it must be okay. I applied, tested to qualify and enlisted. Who took me to "Whitehall Street" in New York City to be sworn in? Dick and Arax, of course. Immediately after delivering me to the Army, Dick delivered himself to the hospital for an emergency appendectomy. Dick never said a word to me about his discomfort. My brother was more concerned on not compounding my pre-induction jitters. Typical Dick.

Once in the Army, I had the opportunity to select and study a language (Russian) for one year at the Army Language School in Monterey, California. In a letter Dick wrote to me "forget crypto – be a linguist." Again, it was the right move. Dick was uncanny in his foresight.

In December of 1951, I flew home on Christmas break from my studies at the Language School. To my great joy I met Dick and Arax's newborn baby, "Richard Haig" the first of our family's next generation. I was especially honored to act as his Godfather a few days after Christmas. Happily the circumstances would recur in 1954 and 1957 as I was again privileged to christen Kenneth Armen and Carol Susan.

After returning to Monterey that winter I was visited by my sister Mary. Together we trained down to Los Angeles where we were honored, once again, to baptize cousins Souren and Annig's first born, Diane. Actually Diane was the first American-Armenian of the second generation born to the Sergenian clan.

It was a cold day in January of 1954 when I returned to my base in Geissen Germany after a one week furlough in Paris. In camp I was delighted to find official instructions ordering me to ship home. The orders were some two months earlier than expected. My discharge date was March 15th, but Uncle Sam was giving me a belated Christmas present. I quickly wrote three or four letters and post dated them for the next ten days. I gave instructions to a friend when to mail them. What I was attempting to do was to trick the folks back home (so they would not worry about my winter Atlantic crossing) and have them believe I was still in Germany awaiting orders. When my ship (the General Eltinge) docked at Staten Island, New York on a frosty and frigid morning two weeks later, I was astounded to see amidst the cheering crowd, someone holding a large sign reading "Welcome Home Haigy." I could not believe there was another Armenian on board, and his name was Haig, just like mine! When I got a better look it was Dick waving the sign flanked by Mary and Mom at his side. I had never figured that their letters to me would be returned with information regarding my current status. Never try to fool Bro, Sis, Mom or Dad.

Pop was not feeling well so he remained home but Mom, Dick and Mary braved the cold early January morn to come greet me. Dick and Mary took the day off from work to be there. What a family.

A few days later I was Honorably Discharged from the Army and who do you think was at the gate at Camp Kilmer, New Jersey to bring me home. Dick, of course. We first drove to Palisades Park,

New Jersey where I was welcomed by Arax, reunited with toddler Richie and introduced to Ken. After lunch Dick drove me home to reconnect with the rest of the family, Mom, Pop, and Mary, to hug and kiss and start anew. Dick eased my return to Pictorial Engraving and I believe he talked to the owners, Mr. Edwards and Mr. Onnig, securing my place in turn for an apprenticeship. Gaining membership into an "elite" trade union was a much valued opportunity. Acquiring a lifetime skill would assure me of a reliable and rewarding financial future. Dick was there; he was now laying the groundwork for me once again.

In the summer of 1954 the Engravers Union was offering a scholarship in Graphic Arts for any son or brother of a union member. A four year scholarship at Columbia University was the highly prized plum of this competition. Each applicant was required to submit a transcript of their previous academic grades, and then compete in a series of intense and diverse examinations. There would be only one winner, only one scholarship.

Again Dick encouraged me to apply. My high school averages certainly did not qualify me for a school as prestigious as Columbia but I did have a knack of testing well. I had also graded superior at the Army Language School. The competition was fierce with more than two hundred qualified applicants. Fortunately I did test well but unfortunately did not receive the grant. Instead I was informed by the registrar at Columbia (not the Engravers Union), that I had scored exceptionally well and the University offered me admittance under the G.I. Bill if I could maintain a B minus average for a period of 30 credit hours.

For the next eight years, at night, I studied at "Morningside Heights" and maintained a grade average well above the registrar's benchmark. Monterey had taught me well on how to prepare and compete on a high level. I never completed my studies or received my degree. I fell some twenty credits short before I opted for marriage to my dream princess and joining Dick in a business partnership. But again, Dick's advice and encouragement enabled me to gain a wonderful experience and education at Columbia University. Decades later all five of my brother's and my offspring have achieved their degrees and then complimented them with graduate degrees and honors. Dick had much to do in influencing all the family's youngsters to covet higher education, as he did to me, years earlier.

During the next brace of years a number of events occurred further cementing the relationship between brothers. Dick bought his home in River Edge, New Jersey. About the same time Mom, Pop, Mary and I bought our first car. We shared the happy newness of these moments together. Actually Dick insisted I drive the new '54 Ford home myself from the dealership. It was nighttime, some five miles from our apartment and I did not yet have a license.

So with Dick and Mary next to me I managed to drive home. Whew!

At Pictorial Engraving I was having some difficulty in getting my chance at an apprenticeship. Mr. Edwards had promised his nephew the "next opening," bypassing my time on the job. Apprenticeships were granted by agreement between the union and ownership. Since there had been "an open door" for apprenticeships for returning G.I.s after World War II the apprentice "roles" of the union were overfilled. New memberships were hard to come by and this squeeze of apprenticeship opportunities frequently led to bribes of union officials.

When my status at Pictorial became precarious Dick explored the possibility of leaving Pictorial and taking a job with a non-union shop (at a much lower salary). His reasoning was that he had information of the prospect of that shop soon becoming Union. The ownership would then guarantee that I would get their first apprenticeship. Fortunately the scheme was too shaky and Dick stayed at Pictorial. Just the thought of Dick taking such a major risk for me is an indication of his boundless and sometimes groundless devotion. If anything Dick was too giving for his own good. Sometimes his benevolence clouded his judgment. He always thought he could find a way to help.

It was in December of '56 I believe, when Dick had a horrendous accident at the shop. While working at the two-color press on a rush overtime job late in the evening, Dick's right hand became caught in the press rollers. In screaming pain, Dick dashed across the traffic at 34th Street and 8th Avenue with me at his side. He ran into the offices of a "compensation doctor" we used for emergency help. Dick had wrapped his crushed fingers in an ink and blood drenched cloth. The doctor did his best to clean the damaged digits and was successful in stemming the gushing flow of blood. He then called French Hospital and arranged for Dick's admittance.

During the one to two hour emergency procedure in the office Dick was in excruciating pain, screaming for Arax, his Mom, for his Dad, for me. I don't know if he received any pain killers, but if he did, they did little to help. Together we took a taxi for the few blocks to the hospital. Dick was shaking and moaning in shock. I half carried him into the Emergency Room and stayed until he was admitted to a room. Dick asked me to go to his home and explain to Arax what had happened. This was one of the most difficult tasks ever asked of me.

Dick lost parts of three fingers on his right hand, and spent weeks in and out of hospitals during the next six months. Plastic surgery was performed at Harkness Pavilion, Columbia Presbyterian Hospital in New York City. His crushed fingers took time to heal because of recurrent infection which resulted from the inks and other chemicals used by pressmen. Dick of course recovered but the sights and sounds of that night will never be forgotten.

In June of 1957 I was finally granted an apprenticeship. I had worked at Pictorial for eleven years. I was now twenty-six years old and, at last, had reached my goal. Unbeknownst to me, Dick had become involved in the shadowy dealings of "union payoffs." The Business Agent of the Union had made it clear to my brother and to Mr. Edwards that naught would take place until "green caressed his palm." I'm still not sure of the details, but I have heard that Dick "donated" one thousand dollars, and Mr. Edwards a like amount. Later Dick "compensated" Mr. Edwards for his "contribution." Two thousand dollars in 1957 when the "take home" for a journeyman was less than two hundred dollars a week was a hefty load to carry.

Another incident during that general time period occurred and influenced my journey through life. In the middle and late fifties I earned somewhere between forty and fifty dollars a week. I lived at home, worked at Pictorial and traveled back and forth to Columbia three nights a week. My social life, what little I had, was with my non-Armenian friends whom I had known since I was a pre-teenager. Most of them were former Boy Scouts from our local Troop. We had formed a club called "The High Hatters." We bowled, played ball, fished, hung out and, on occasion, had dances and parties. We collected dues to cover the cost of these affairs.

One of our rules was – no date- no admittance to the party. Sadly, I was not always socially astute and missed many a dance and party. But I did my best to date when possible.

One day Pop shocked me to the quick when he announced in his formal fatherly voice, "Haig, if you do not 'take' (marry) an Armenian girl you will not be my son." I know he did not mean he would "disown" me. I rationalized his message indicated that I would drift away from the family. Remember, there was an intense and necessary "clansmanship" of Armenians in Moslem Turkey. This protective cloak had changed little in America. But not knowing exactly what Pop's intent was, or what I needed to do, I sought Dick's advice. Dick again was gentle but succinct. He translated and reformed Pop's law to mean, "Haig you can find happiness with any girl you chose but you probably will be more comfortable, as will we, if you chose a girl from a similar culture and background."

Examining this last paragraph, I think I have "tweaked" and paraphrased my brother's words, but hopefully you will get the meaning.

A few years later when I was financially a bit more stable, Mary Kachian, my life's mate and I discovered each other. Fortunately for me Mary surpassed my father's criteria as well as exceeded my own.

I am so blessed to have had a wonderful bro- and for sixty years we called each other that name –

pronounced bro- as in brother not bro as in broken. I am so blessed because he guided me, encouraged me and showed me with unimagined opportunities. Dick seldom if ever demanded, insisted or executed his claim upon the course of my actions.

If I did not heed my Pop's words regarding marriage, I am sure I would have had the love and support of the whole family, and all would have turned out alright. But it seems my fate was written on my forehead. I could not see it but Dick did! In September of 1962 Dick held the Holy Cross over my head and the head of my bride Mary as we became one. We wed at the same altar, in the same church, as did Dick and Arax in 1950, Mary's parents Mgrditch and Rahan in 1930, and Avedis and Ardemis in 1921.

Dick was my best man in 1962, for all the year preceding the ceremony, and then again for all the years since.

Nineteen sixty two was a hallmark year for another reason. The partners at Pictorial Engraving offered Dick an 1/4 share of the company. Dick was going to become a partner! At that time the company was owned by Mr. Edwards, his son Eddie Junior and Sam Vosganian. All held twenty-five percent shares.

I cannot attest to the following, but I absolutely believe that Dick insisted that I (still serving my apprenticeship) be included in the partnership. He was willing to split his share in two to assure my future. Since I was ineligible to become an owner as an apprentice it was agreed that the split would be announced only after I reached the status of "journeyman" one year later. When Dick told me of the offer to bring us in as partners I was uneasy and hesitant. The shop had not been doing well and it seemed a dangerous and expensive risk. Dick quelled my fears by again shooting straight, no B.S. "we will probably never get rich, but we will always have a job at Pictorial." Once again, in my life, Dick had wielded the proverbial trowel and applied the mortar to set the cornerstone of my financial future.

In 1965 and again in 1966 Mary and I were supremely blessed with a daughter, Nadine and then a son, Michael. Again Dick was the right man as he stood reverently as Godfather for both.

On January 6, 1967 our father Avedis passed away suddenly and quietly, in his sleep. He died of a heart attack. He died on his name day "Avedis," (which translates to "Good News"), also the religious celebration of Armenian Christmas. It was the first death in the Sarajian family in four decades and we were all overcome with grief. Dick now assumed the role of patriarch, the oldest and wisest male. Of course, Dick never sought any role or rank above another. In my own mind's eye Dick's compassion and boundless love was the most precious inherent gift he derived from Avedis.

For the rest of our special relationship as brothers, partners and best friends I perceived Dick as our family's "Good Sheppard." His benevolence was always available to all he touched. In our family or with friends, in our Church, social or business functions Dick stood out as the "good guy," "Uncle Dick," "Aghbar Dick," "Unger Dick," "DiDi Dick" and most of all, for those who knew him best, "Hokis Dick."

Dick was also known as the "peacemaker," the voice of compromise and reason. In Armenian politics he was a bridge between feuding ideologies. In church affairs Dick was even more effective. Besides being one of the original "Pillars" of Sts. Vartanantz, he was the architect of our Church Basketball League. Dick's perception of inter-church activities facilitated Diocese-Prelacy harmony. He disregarded verbal jibes from both sides and acted as the flux that helped smooth out petty differences and even outright hostility between opposing factions of the fledgling basketball league. The result was more than the inception of inter-church basketball. Dick's foresight affected an athletic brotherhood conceived to heal decades of discord. While those few near-sighted Board Members of Prelacy and Diocese parishes wallowed in years of distrust, Dick not only introduced sports- but sportsmanship into the lives of our Armenian youth. His vision was to help salve old wounds through the interplay of their children.

Dick was among the first advisor to the A.Y.F. youth in New York and he was the man of choice as he and his wife Arax served for many years nourishing the minds and spirits of our Sunday School children as head administrators.

In the business world Dick often defused battles between piqued salesmen or dire differences between union leaders and management. Dick was effective, succinct, uncomplicated. In his dealings with his own children who can forget Ken Sarajian's poignant, tearful recollections during the Memorial Dinner following Dick's Funeral Service. One revealing yet humorous tale spun by Ken dealt with Dick's decision to finally have a "man to man" with his "boy." Dick and Arax were driving Ken, away from the safety of the nest into the perils of college life. Dick had remained unusually silent until the car approached the boundaries of staid old Franklin and Marshall College in Lancaster, Pennsylvania. It was there Dick sternly reminded Ken not to forget that his actions reflected upon the reputation and honor of the Sarajian name. Dick then followed with these memorable words, "REMEMBER KEN, THERE ARE GOOD GIRLS AND BAD GIRLS."

During the ensuing years my memories meld together in a happy haze highlighted by holiday celebrations. Christmas Eve was always at Dick and Arax's home. Together as one family we also rejoiced "en-masse" during birthdays, anniversaries, graduations and festive holidays (Fourth of July on the lawn at Dick's). We reveled during family reunions or just laughed during ordinary "kef" (fun) times. We shared all the good moments and helped dry each other's tears at our sorrows.

Somehow Dick seemed to be in the center of family life. But don't get me wrong, Dick was not always right; he was not "perfect." I think it only fair that I now expose a few flaws in my brother's character. Dick's nature was so "undefiled" that he believed, (really, really, believed), that some of his loved ones (family or friends) could not do any wrong. Not everyone mind you, but more than just a few! For those closest to him, his wife and his children, he did notice "indiscretions" but he was always able to forgive and forget all their errors.

For a select group, for some reason Dick would hold them totally blameless, sinless and guiltless, no matter the circumstances or proof. This observation by Dick tended to chide and chaff many who were closest to Dick. Among the first of the "anointed ones" was brother Haig, (me), and cousin Souren. By some sacred sanction or miracle, our transgressions were forgiven and forgotten before they even occurred.

Sam was Dick's brother, if not by birth-by sheer love. He was unique, compelling and very special. His extraordinary talents and effusive, ebullient spirit were sadly preordained to be tarnished if not diminished by the human conditions of over-use of tobacco and alcohol. Perhaps it was the cruel effects of the war, or perhaps it was Souren's own stretch for perfection. Even Souren's charms were intoxicating. Souren seemed designated by fate to be our family prize, our shimmering star. Instead, in time, he was fated to fall to weaknesses. But no matter how tainted or blemished, his radiance endured in Dick's vista and my brother's lifelong pledge of loyalty, support and love never faltered. Souren was a favorite!

As for me, permit me now to re-expose a nearly forgotten scenario. It was in the '70's, late fall and we are in Dick's backyard. We (Rich, Ken and my son Michael, then about eleven or twelve years old), started a game of football. The game pitted Rich and me against Ken and Michael. Ken, I believe, was "conditioning" for his senior year on the wrestling team at River Dell High. He was a tough and solid 175 lbs. The game started out as "touch" football, but soon degraded to sloppy, floppy "tackle." On one play Ken caught a pass and was tackled and held by brother Rich. I came in and "finished the job." Ken collapsed writhing in pain, his wrestling season all but gone. Dick heard the screams of agony and came rushing out. Dick listened to our frantic and graphic description and explanation of what happened. (I don't recall if it was a torn leg muscle or sprained ankle). When all the facts were clear and Ken was preparing for a trip to the Emergency Room, Dick finally spoke and scolded his son Rich for not being more careful. Not one word was uttered to me – the real culprit.

Through the years, at times I have been kidded and teased about this special relationship I shared with Dick. I never felt embarrassed, or guilty, or even unfairly privileged by our bond. It just was! Dick was <u>so</u> good, I almost took him for granted.
Sure, now as I look back, I realize how fortunate I was. We were a team. He was always giving and I did much of the getting.

Certainly at one time, when I was much younger, I was critical and, at times, unfairly faulted Mom and Pop for being too strict. (I guess all kids say that). Mom and Pop always spoke that "other language" and made us speak it too. And in our mailbox we would get that newspaper with all those funny symbols. It would always embarrass me. My sister Mary always studied and did her homework with the radio playing music. Dick he was different. He was fun and I could talk to him and he would really listen. Sometime he knew what I was thinking before I said it. I always felt he understood me and for a kid, it's important to be understood. Dick was casual, smooth, natural, and really ordinary. He was so ordinary he was extra-ordinary. Now I can say it, he was extraordinary. I got the sense that no one ever felt "gifted" by Dick. Blessed, yes, but you never felt you owed him. No repayment was in order. No I.O.U. That was just the way Dick was, that was my brother.

When I think back, Dick's "secret work" in intelligence during World War II had a holdover effect. My brother seemed to have developed a special skill regarding the release of information including information specifically about his own health issues. His approach was either to minimize the condition or hide it completely. When I queried him – "Why, Dick??" he would smile, chuckle and change the subject. I guess he did not want to share any of his pain with anyone else. And many times, in many ways, he was even able to draw humor out of his hurt.

Dick also displayed a penchant for sustaining an illness or injury immediately before an important personal or family event. I will mention a few, but be sure, there were many.

Dick and I were attending a "Board of Trade" Convention with our partners and other shop owners. The site was Rochester, New York. Unbeknownst to me (or anyone else) Dick was suffering from an impacted wisdom tooth. At the hotel we were fortunate to all have separate rooms. Sometime after midnight the pain in Dick's jaw became unbearable. My brother, unable to find a cab, walked to the nearest hospital (about a mile) and asked for help. They gave him some pain killer shots and hooked him up with an antibiotic I.V. The next morning he took a cab back to the hotel and conferred with Andy Shahinian, (another shop owner). Dick knew Andy was planning an early return so he made arrangements to exit Rochester with him. He did not contact me or our partners but left a short note with a sanitized version of the night's events. Another secret mission completed. Andy drove Dick directly to the Dentist where the "unwise" wisdom tooth was extracted.

I vaguely recall, again many years ago, Dick suffering severe chest discomfort as he was boarding a plane to Bermuda. It was the start of one of Dick and Arax's rare vacations. Happily it passed quickly and was not as serious as it appeared.

Who could forget Dick's splash down with an acid bath at work a week prior to his son Richard's graduation from Colgate University. Dick had been hospitalized with severe arm, leg and torso burns from the nitric acid but nevertheless insisted on signing out of the hospital and driving to distant Hamilton, New York for the ceremony. He was back in the hospital with a festering infection right after the return trip home. It was years later (1997) when Dick attended Nadine and Greg's wedding in a wheelchair after another long bout in the hospital. Carol's husband Jim was Dick's wheelchair chauffeur. At the reception Dick was too weak to walk, no less to dance but never too weak to smile.

The day before the scheduled gala celebration of Dick and Arax's Fiftieth Anniversary, Dick fell at home, broke his nose, cut and blackened his eye. But there he was, present and reporting for duty, alongside his devoted Arax. At the restaurant Dick was so engrossed with greeting, hugging and laughing with his guests he appeared to pay no mind to his discomforts.

Even when Dick was crowned King, that is King of the A.Y.F. Olympics, his neck was garnished with a brace. The uncomely device was a reminder of the serious disc surgery Dick had undergone a week earlier. Even "stiff necked" Dick's kingly countenance was aglow with a regal presence and a noble smile.

When our venerable Rahan Kachian died in February 2006, Dick weakened and wracked by years of pain, still found the inner strength to attend every religious service. Dick was always "on call." He never took time off. Being there was not a sacrifice for Dick, it was a calling.

After Dick's retirement in 1991 he met and withstood a myriad of serious medical issues. His longtime battle with arthritis of the spine took almost a foot off his once proud and erect six foot stature. In its place the crippling disease left a mile of pain behind for Dick to deal with. His sure and athletic gait was reduced to a shuffle and then to a slow motion hobble. But he always tried, God knows he never quit, never did he say enough is enough!

The childhood scourge of rheumatic fever which had hospitalized him as a teenager re-erupted in Dick's senior years and exposed its decades of damage. In its aftermath it destroyed Dick's kidneys. During his final ten years, Dick was relegated to alternating days of kidney dialysis. The procedure put a serious "crimp" on the lives of both Dick and Arax, but their attitude, their devotion to each other never diminished, only strengthened. Perhaps Dick leaned on Arax a bit more but she was always, always willing to carry the burden.

The couple endured surgeries of a triple coronary bypass and the insertion of a metal plate to stabilize a broken pelvis (for Dick) and two hip replacements (for Arax). Their retirement years were not uneventful. During his last years you could gauge the ebbing of Dick's wonderful reservoir of strength and dogged determination. Both his sight and hearing dimmed but not his spark, never his spirit. True his vision faded, but the gleam in the corner of Dick's eyes shone with his "joy for life." A joy he was always prepared to share, if not give away freely.

On a bright and sunny July 8th of the year 2006, my nephew Ken phoned my home and told my wife Mary that he needed to come and "bounce something off me". When he came, he came with Jim (his brother-in-law), and Arax. Mary foresaw some impending and distressing news. Ken and Jim came down to my basement (my usual lair) and when our eyes met all words were superfluous.

Dick had collapsed during dialysis and could not be revived. Just like that an era passed, a legend passed, my brother, my hokis brother passed. The three of us went upstairs to the living room where we wept as a group. Along with Arax, Rich and Carol had come. We made efforts of consoling each other, and deep inside I felt blessed and so honored that the family chose to surround me, here at my home, where we would comfort each other. The next few days still remain a blur to me. The outpouring of the community was overwhelming. Ken eulogized his father with emotion and devotion. He noted in tearful humor that now Dick once again stood his full six feet plus in height and was finally devoid of pain as he walked to the Heavenly Gate.

At the funeral service a message from His Holiness, Catholicos Aram the First, recalled Vehapar's early encounters with Dick and praised Dick not only for a lifetime of good deeds, but a humility that glorified his works.

At the burial Dick found his final resting place alongside Yeghishe and Satenig Catchouny. His grave was blessed and consecrated with the soil and waters from his father's village of Efkere and his mother's city of Shabin Karahisar.

At the Memorial Dinner, Ken again spoke and his words evoked tears not only from the mourners, but in profusion from Ken himself. Lastly Richard, the first born, spoke and touched all with his quiet eloquence and his tenderness. He said that the most glowing tribute to Dick was illustrated by the love that was showered upon us, his family, during the past three days. A love which we understood was always meant for Dick.

My own words remained silent in my throat. I thought of many things, episodes and happenings I could share, but somehow I felt my time with Dick was special, almost sacred to only the two of us. My words then, as probably now, would lack the strength of the knot that bound us as brothers. Dick never needed praise, least of all from me.

One passage of words did grip and enthrall us all. They were gracefully and sincerely offered by His Eminence Archbishop Oshagan Choloyan. The Prelate, officiating at the Funeral service, eulogized Dick in warm, endearing terms which were fraught with his own emotions. His normally deep and resonant voice seemed softened by the Archbishop's gentle embrace of the moment. With thought and care he composed a sublime word picture which I shall always cherish and preserve as the prayerful memorial to Dick. His Eminence pictured my loving brother taken by hand, with Divine care by our Lord Jesus. Our Savior was showing Dick the way, guiding him safely through the Valley of Death and toward the light.

Archbishop Choloyan completed his "spoken portrait" of Dick's fate with a few last loving strokes. His final account described Dick being presented to our Heavenly Father by His Son. The Prelate's vision, his portrayal was not assembled with paints, or even words. His canvas was covered with pure light. It was the light of hope and faith and the promise of eternal life.

God knows us all by name, but what sweetness it must be when He calls you into His Kingdom. Christ's last words upon the Cross were "It is finished." So too was Dick's time here on earth. And as we believe – IT IS ONLY THE BEGINNING.

B. My Sister Mary

The American landscape offered the post-Genocide survivors much more than freedom and sanctuary. The "American Dream" was not gossamer thin or puppy-tail fancy, it was real. Opportunities abounded, not only to salve the spirit of a ravaged race but to expand the horizon for their children. The stepping stone for most first generation American-Armenians was education.

Dick and I had an educational advantage over Mary as a result of our military service. The "GI Bill" afforded every veteran a four-year college education. The GI Bill was probably the best investment Uncle Sam ever made. It provided to what was later called the "Greatest Generation" the broadest spectrum of higher education ever offered. Its dividends would spurn America into "Super Nationhood."

Without the benefits of the GI Bill, Mary's studies ended at high school. My sister was more than qualified to attend college. Indeed, she had been skipped twice during her grade school years and she completed high school in three years. She was graduated at the top of her class from Grover Cleveland High School a few weeks past her 16th birthday; she was not just smart, she was a whiz!

She entered the working force at 16 and never looked back. At Mary's last job (which lasted more than 20 years), her skill and dedication was much valued. She was the Personal Executive Assistant to Martin Coleman. Mr. Coleman was the son-in-law of the heir to Mosler family. Mosler Safe Company was one of the most prestigious corporations in American Industry.

For her entire lifetime, Mary embraced the role of family communicator. She visited, corresponded with and phoned members of our family and friends. People would seek out Mary to converse, communicate, gossip and exchange the latest news. Mary was always available, unpretentious, warm and sharing. She would listen and not lecture. She never missed birthdays, anniversaries and holidays.

Mary was always available to relatives and friends. She was totally committed to my parents' wants and needs. Besides being the family's source of income for more than 50 years, Mary did all of the little things as well. She was seldom noticed but always there.

During my time at Columbia, she would type, edit and correct my assignments. Her unselfish and giving nature may well have stemmed from her DNA. Generation One got more than just life from the survivors, many of us were blessed with the moral fiber and ethics of our parents as well.

As a pre-adolescent, I really admired my big brother and sister. I guess it was part of the age difference. They were eight and six years older than me and were teenagers for most of my earliest memories. Dick was my hero, but Mary was more complex. She exhibited a dual nature, a dichotomy of spirits. On one hand, she was quiet, serious and respectful and even bordered on timid. She was a typical 1930s girl of Armenian refugee parents. But somehow you could sense a fearless streak in her. She harbored a stubborn intensity in her five foot one inch frame.

Before I was ten years old, Mary was sixteen and worked full time in Manhattan. She loved the excitement of traveling daily by subway to the city. Even as a young teenager, Mary loved visiting those elegant, cathedral-like movie theaters in the City. The movie palaces of that era always featured a live stage show along with a first-run film. Mary bubbled with pleasure as she retold her adventures of standing in line at the Paramount Theater for hours and then watching Frank Sinatra in person croon his way into every girl's heart. Mary wasn't always sedate, she was a boisterous bobby-soxer!

At the onset of World War II, after Dick and Souren had gone off to fight, Mary "hounded" my parents for their permission to join the women's naval service (the "Waves"). My parents were not about to send a second child off to war. Nevertheless, Mary's demands became moot when my father suffered his first heart attack and Mary became the sole supporter of our family. Barely 20 years old and she kept our family afloat.

Mary was also a stalwart supporter of my activities. When she heard that I had qualified to take the entrance examination to Brooklyn Technical High School, one of four scholarship high schools in NY, she encouraged me and prepared me for the entrance exam. She also supported my extra-curricular activities such as boy scouts and stickball. She took me to my first major league baseball game at Ebbetts Field between the Brooklyn Dodgers and the Cincinnati Reds (even though I was a Yankees fan.) We went to Steeplechase Park at Coney Island to ride the rides and spent hours building model airplanes.

Mary's love of travel began with short trips to Boston and Detroit. She next visited California, Mexico and Canada. She traveled with friends Alice Vemian, Alice Hamparian Kasparian, the Manoogian sisters Ann and Jessie, Roxie Sookikian, Laura Zappala and Arpy Kashmanian. They visited Italy, France, the British Isles, Greece, and Monaco, the Caribbean, Alaska, the Panama Canal and the South American coast. Mary visited Armenia with me, my wife Mary and Mom Kachian. It was a memorable and treasured visit for all of us, not only because of what we saw or did but because of the moments we shared in each other's company. I can still see the four of us in the wondrous glow of the majestic Mt. Ararat.

In my mother's later years, she escorted Mom to a tearful reunion with Mom's elder sister Aghavni in California. It took this visit and this space in time for the two exiles from Shabin Karahisar to share their darkest secrets of their years in Turkish repression. Seventy years had passed and Mom had never told her sister about the death march out of Tamzara or the tragic death of their sister Victoria and her two babies. Aghavni had never shared with Mom the story of the death of her husband in Tokat and the loss of their youngest sibling Souren. They were ashamed and guilty. Neither realized that the guilt and shame belonged to the Ottomans and was never their own.

Mary was not privy to the two sisters' conversation until much later. The two surviving brothers, Kaloust and Andon, never heard their sisters' confessions. They were too painful to share.

Some of Mary's firsts were not totally happy in nature. She was the first to feel the touch of a surgeon's scalpel. Shortly after I was born, Mary was stricken with mastoiditis. This infection involves the area behind the ear and very close to the brain. In the 1930s, an operation was the only treatment and it was a life-threatening procedure. Mary recovered but a deep cavity behind her ear was her souvenir for life. Mom and Pop's reminder was overcoming yet another bout with life and death.

A few years later, Mary underwent surgery for a lazy eye lid. The cure is corrective slicing of the eyelid. Again, a gamble for Mary and my parents, as the outcome depended on the skill of the surgeon. Fortunately, the surgery was a success.

A third of the firsts happened in the early 1940s. Mom, Mary and I were visiting Uncle Kaloust and his family in Boston. One evening, Mary was stricken with intense abdominal pain. A doctor was called and diagnosed appendicitis. An ambulance was summoned to take Mary to Massachusetts General Hospital. The things I remember from that point on, in order, are first- Mom was almost hysterical in grief. Second, Uncle Kaloust trying in vain to contact Pop in Brooklyn (we had no phone at home). Third, Morak and the girls instructing Mary to give their address as her home and not Brooklyn. They were afraid that Mass General would refuse to treat a Brooklyn native.

Fortunately, all turned out well. Mom eventually calmed down, Pop got the call at the local drug store's phone booth and rushed to Boston and a young surgeon removed Mary's appendix. My parents' reaction to this surgery was an indication of how fragile my parents' psyche was and how deep their scars from the Ottomans were; they considered another loss unbearable.

Prior to entering Hackensack Hospital just before she died, Mary spent the week at our house. She was too weak to be left alone. Tearful goodbyes were exchanged between my wife Mary, Mom Kachian and Mary. I drove my sister to her haven in Hackensack. Her condo in the Jefferson Towers was the only home Mary had ever owned. It was her little piece of paradise in Bergen County.

Her apartment was meticulous, not a thing out of place or awry- the way she always kept it. We only stayed for minutes as she gathered what she needed for her "short" hospital stay. When I noticed some dried out plants and offered to water them, Mary quipped, "just toss them." She made no mention of getting replacements. Those were her last words in what had been her home for almost ten years.

We left for the hospital and in an agonizing week's time, she was gone. We never saw the end coming. I felt she was stolen from the family. Our Memik was gone.

I'm sure we all harbor deep fears about who will sort through our possessions when we die. Mary made it easy for us. Her nieces, Carol and Nadine and her nephews Rich, Ken and Michael had the difficult task of going through her lifetime's belongings. They all had the same thought, "her planning made it so physically easy for us but her preparations pained her loss all the more."

As I fumbled for the right words at her Memorial Luncheon, I said something about her caring and loving manner. I noted that she was never angry or demeaning in any way. Now, though, I am saddened to admit, especially as one so close to her, that I never did realize her "halo." Why is it that those who are the best amongst us are often taken for granted? Mary's gift was that she absorbed the best that Avedis and Ardemis had to give. A little bit of Mom's reserve and caution and a little bit of Pop's brash exuberance. She was the best of the next generation; the link that solidified our family chain.

If you want a glimpse of her spirit, her essence and how she radiated love to all, turn to the page of prose Mary chose as her farewell message. Nadine read it at her wake, haltingly and with many tears and swallowed sobs. That was our "Memik."

The photograph that brought my father to tears: Dikran and
Mariam Sarajian together with Avedis' first wife Vartouhi, his
daughter Mariam and his nephew, 1914, Efkere

Efkere c. 1900 (above) and Soorp Stepanos Church,
Efkere, c. 1910 (below)

The author at Soorp Stepanos Church, Efkere, 1998 (above) and Shabin Karahisar (below) with the Pert in the background, c.1913

The author with Archbishop Mesrop Ashjian and Nubar
Zoryan in Shabin Karahisar (above) and with the Pert in the
background (below), 1998

The Sergenians reunite in Constantinople, 1919. Ardemis and
Kaloust in the rear and Andon and Aghavni in the foreground

Ardemis Sergenian, 1919, Constantinople

Souren and Kaloust Sergenian, 1914, Tokat

Avedis Sarajian (on right), 1914, New York, NY

Avedis and Ardemis (Sergenian) Sarajian, October 16, 1921,
New York, NY

Aghavni (Sergenian) and Mirijan Dermengian, January 8,
1921, Syracuse, New York

Andon and Shoushan (Chahinian) Sardjenian, August 29,
1923, Athens, Greece

Kaloust and Keghanoush (Agababian) Sergenian (engagement
photo), 1925, Brockton, Massachusetts

Ardemis and Avedis Sarajian with Dikran, Mary and Haig,
June 1936, Brooklyn, New York

Der Hoosig Hazarian Catchouny

The Beads of Changri, 2008, courtesy of Krikor Pidedjian

Satenig and
Yeghishe
Catchouny, 1923
(above) and
General Antranik
Ozanian, c. 1919,
(on right)

Professor Mardiros Delerian, c. 1910 (above) and Dick Sarajian, Archbishop Mesrop Ashjian and Rahan Kachian during Surpazan's last visit to our home in November 2003 (below)

Three generations: Kohar and Garabed Kachian together with Rahan and Mgrditch and their children, Mary, Berjouhi and Mardig, 1938, New York

Rahan (Delerian) Kachian and Mgrditch Kachian, 1929,
New York

Chapter 22

The Khnamies (The In-Laws)

More Stories of Survival

A short time after I completed the story of my parents' lives I felt the need to at least touch upon the experiences of their khnamies, the Catchounys and the Kachians. Yeghishe and Satenig Catchouny, and Mgrditch and Rahan Kachian were among the few that withstood and survived the tempest of Turkish annihilation of the Armenians in 1915. Their story is, in substance, analogous to Avedis' and Ardemis' saga and almost a template of half a million other tales which filtered out of Turkey early in the last century.

My desire to incorporate and record the Khnamies' story in this narrative serves two purposes. First, it will provide for the family a written extract of two extraordinary couples and their will to survive. I am (we are) fortunate to be able to draw upon written documents, audio and video recordings along with a lifetime of a loving relationships to recapture the voices of these four survivors. As an adjunct to these pages of our family "diary," the Catchouny's and the Kachian's harrowing tales of escape will help punctuate the commonality of the Armenian Experience during the declining years of the Ottoman Empire. How often have we, their heirs, assembled and examined fragments of our exiled survivors' history and marveled as we compared stories of undeniable similarity fraught with the sameness of circumstances and happenstance.

The rhythms of our diasporite history occur, reoccur and then concur over and over again in a terrible tangled tale. More than two million Armenians were summoned in Turkey to stage this 1915 drama – this tragedy. And this "Act" had but a single theme, just one script for all. It would be called for the first time – GENOCIDE.

Months ago as I labored to carefully assemble the material I needed to relate the "Khnamie" episodes I was astounded by the frequency of recurring coincidences. Be aware and you will surely recognize the parallels of their lives as you read on.

The recurrence of similarity between the Catchounys and Kachians is evident as they journeyed across Anatolia and crossed the Atlantic.

Among Armenians the word "khnamie" both implies and expresses a warmer and more intimate definition from its translated version of "in-law" in English. Often, the in-laws refer to each other as khnamie or perhaps khnamie followed by a first name. The emphasis is upon the relationship rather than the given name. This approach, at least to me, designates a special affection and significance. Just the word "khnamie" promotes a permanence of relationships between the families. Not only have the bride and groom wed at the ceremonial altar, but all their families are bonded as well. The respect, warmth and love between the Sarajians and their khnamies were a stalwart foundation which their children could embrace and rely upon. Certainly this relationship influenced my desire to include their stories following the pages of my parent's lives. However, I had another compelling purpose for recording and honoring their lives within this narrative. The drama of the Catchounys and Kachians and their stirring deeds have given me the opportunity to examine the "uncommon valor" of the Armenians in 1915 Turkey. In such an exposition I find myself drawn to the riveting truth on how pervasive and absolutely routine was this annihilation of all Armenians in early 20th Century Turkey. This was a total and complete plan and effort to purge. It was a coordinated nationwide expulsion and was loosely disguised as an effort to insure internal security. However, its results give proof to its true purpose. Its aim was to end the Armenian habitation in Turkey, regardless of the loss of life.

As I resume this narrative and delve into the lives and times of the Catchounys and the Kachians, I believe that you will begin to recognize many of the similarities and coincidences. Perhaps you will remember your own survivor's tale. You will probably note each anguish and torment and compare it with one suffered by a survivor in your family. You will smile and glow with each escape, each victory and success then look for its counterpart and then celebrate as they did! Each scene, every situation and episode in their saga helps give testimony and then proof to the scope of the ethnic carnage in 1915, and then elevates and glorifies our ancestors' stubborn struggle to overcome.

I trust that you, in your own moments of peaceful reverie, will not forget to remember them. And when you do, multiply their tales of heartbreak and times of triumph by each of the half million survivors of 1915. These were our legendary "Silent Generation." Perhaps now you can begin to understand the breadth of their experiences and the depth of their sorrow.

Chapter 23

The Catchounys and the Gorgodians

On Sunday evening December 7, 1941, my parents Avedis and Ardemis, my brother Dick and my sister Mary and I were returning from a traditional Armenian gathering called a "Hantes." These festive happenings usually included food, drink and of course an Armenian band. A "hantes" could be held for any number of reasons - or for no reason at all. There were two or three large ballrooms in Manhattan that were popular and usual locations.

I'm not positive, but do believe that this "fall frolic" was held at Webster Hall. I have little recall of this hantes, probably because as a youngster (I was just eleven years old), I never truly enjoyed accompanying my family (not that I had any choice), to those "ethnic" gatherings. But on this one

200

occasion I clearly remember some details of our return trip home. Since we lived in Ridgewood, Queens, the commute from Manhattan required two different subway lines and a walk of about a half-mile.

What I felt that evening was an unusual, stern and somber demeanor about both my mother and father. Somehow my parents had received news about the bombing of Pearl Harbor. I was innocent and unsophisticated in worldly matters. I suppose I thought like any pre-teenager. My mental meanderings were probably typical of any eleven year old. Certainly I was unable to understand the consequences of a war.

On our journey home few if any words were exchanged. I could not help but feel uneasy; a strange silent tension had gripped my parents. Although surrounded by my family, I began to feel scared. I'm sure now that my mother and father understood far better than most Americans what hardships would result from this war. The scars from the Genocide had never healed. Dick and Mary were probably naïve by today's standards of worldly youngsters. However, I am sure that they felt the impending changes and dangers to our lives as well.

Dick was now nineteen and Mary was nearly eighteen. Both were beautiful late teenagers; you know, the age when all kids look great. They were devoted to each other and to the family. How I looked up to my big brother and big sister; they were perfect role models for me. They were loving of family and respectful of adults. They were somewhat guarded and reserved, especially near strangers, as were most Armenian children of this era. The first generation born to our immigrant parents seldom exhibited gregarious, extraverted traits. The terror, heartbreaks and resulting melancholy that resulted from the Genocide followed by the harsh and wanting days of the depression had left the constraints of solemnity upon most of our exiles from Turkey. Their offspring just naturally reflected the mood of their elders.

The outbreak of a war on December 7th served as a stunning shock for all Americans. I am sure that my parents both sensed and feared the changes that were certain to come. As for Dick, Mary and me, the war would impact and influence their lives for at least four years, and for so many others it would change everything forever. Within a short time, no more than a few months, Dick had volunteered and joined the Army Air Corp. He followed the wartime patriotism and passion of his beloved first cousin Souren Dermengian, who had preceded Dick by joining the Army right after December 7th.

Everywhere in America young men and women were rushing to join the military to fight for liberty and freedom. Proud and patriotic parents reluctantly said their tearful goodbyes with the agonizing knowledge that many sons and daughters would never return home. War would be Hell. Glory and honor were the words of journalists. Parents only knew heartache and tears, and for Armenian parents, they were reliving a nightmare.

About twenty miles to the West, across the majestic Hudson River, in an apartment on Main Street in Orange, New Jersey, the Catchounys, now a family of five, also heard the news of the Japanese attack. Yeghishe was fifty-three years old; his wife Satenig was forty-three. The couple had three children. Alice was nineteen, Arax was fourteen and young Armen was six. Yeghishe and Satenig were a part of the "lost" if not "last" generation of Anatolian Armenians. The Catchounys had arrived in America in July of 1922, just weeks before Ardemis Sarajian gave birth to her first son, Dikran. Of course what fate had in store for these two families no one yet knew.

Twenty-five years back in their own storied past, these two native Armenians had also faced the horrors of war. It was certainly a different world in a far different place. Perhaps it was because Yeghishe and Satenig had already been tempered and toughened by the crucible fire of their youth. Together they now bravely accepted their destiny and forged a model, a template of survival for their children. Yet another generation of Armenians was to face the cruel test and trials of war in all its manifestations. Of course 1915 Ottoman Turkey and 1941 America were more than a quantum leap apart. But the legendary genetic trait for survival, so finely honed by the Armenians, stubbornly transcends both time and distance. These ancient people had developed the skills of drawing from our past in order to sustain our future.

Chapter 24

Yeghishe Catchouny

Yeghishe Catchouny was the youngest of four children. His father was Der Hoosig Kahana Hazarian, a village priest. Yeghishe's mother, the Yeretzkin (the title accorded a priest's wife) was Nartouhi (nee Shaboyan). The birth date of Der Hoosig (nee Hagop) was 1851. Nartouhi was probably born around 1860. Yeghishe was born on November 27, 1889 in the village of Arabger (or Arabgir).[25] The town is situated in the central plateau region of Anatolia. It is positioned in the center of the broad Asian peninsula. This land lies between the Black Sea, the Mediterranean Sea, the mountains of the Caucasus and the deserts of Syria, Iran and Iraq. Arabgir is located some thirty or forty miles northwest of the city of Kharpet, which early on in the twentieth century was the district capital of the region. Arabgir, the main or central town, was circled by sixty-eight villyets in 1915. The total population consisted of approximately 10,000 Armenians and 10,000 Muslims. The largest villyet was Tepe, in which seven hundred Armenians lived. Arabgir's industry was mainly comprised of cotton farming and the manufacture of cotton fabrics and threads.[26]

At this point of our story about Yeghishe, permit me to pause and reflect on a personal observation. Arabgir was a fairly large town located only a few miles north of the village of Egin, also called Agin. I am all but certain that this is the very place where my mother Ardemis' fate was touched by what could only have been "Heavenly Intervention." It was here at a temporary encampment along the banks of the rushing waters of the Euphrates where a handful of ragged Armenian exiles awaited their final kismet. They were the meager remnants of what had started out as hundreds of women, children and elderly villagers from Tamzara. Their march to death was almost completed. Their forced sortie nearly reached its prescribed end. Suddenly a Turkish lady of wealthy bearing, a Hannum, rescued Ardemis. She plucked out the bedraggled thirteen year old not because of compassion or pity but for her selfish personal use. Ardemis was the right age to be added among her handmaidens. But not so for Ardemis' sister Victoria and her two babies. For them Agin would be the journey's end. Of course I know you have already read this tragic chapter of Ardemis' life, and probably empathized on how the precious gift of life could also impose such a ponderous burden of guilt upon this innocent girl.

It was because of what happened here and its significance in Ardemis' life that I recognized the "juxtaposition" of place and time. Of Arabgir and Agin, of Yeghishe and Ardemis. I don't believe the two ever discussed the events of this time and place. Rather it is that I, in this writing, am unable to avoid a mental collision with these repeated "chance" occurrences. While writing these narratives I have been teased and tweaked by these little overlaps of destiny. These hidden incidents of fate were my own discoveries, secrets uncovered. I am no longer amazed by similarities.

Chapter 25

Yeghishe's Early Years

Yeghishe's mother died when he was four or five years old.[27] Cholera devastated Arabgir as it did many of the villages in Turkey. Unclean drinking water was the primary cause of its spread and lacking the drugs of today, death was the usual outcome. Anna Sergenian, mother of Ardemis died about the same time in Shabin Karahisar, one hundred miles north of Arabgir.

Yeghishe, now motherless, was cared for by his father, three older brothers and one sister. The senior sibling was Kourken who was born in the late 1870's. His death was reported to be in the mid 1920's. Kourken lived most of his life in Constantinople and was a baker by trade. I have been unable to find any reference to a wife or children. Vrooryr was next in line. He was born in the early

1880s. Again his biography is sketchy, but it appears that Vrooryr had fled Turkey and lived out his days in Canada. Freddy Catchouny, as he was known, died in the mid 1950's. At the time of his death he was residing in Winnipeg, Canada. No other details of his life were available. Marguerite, Yeghishe's sister, was born in 1882 and died in 1965. Marguerite had immigrated to Armenia and married a man named Kevork. The couple had two daughters. The older girl, Nartouhi, later immigrated to the United States and married Setrak Paktikian. Along with their two children, Marguerite and Setrak Jr., Nartouhi and Setrak Sr. resided in New Jersey. Marguerite Paktikian would in 1950 serve as a bridesmaid at the wedding of Dick Sarajian to Arax Catchouny.

After Marguerite (Yeghishe's sister and grandmother to the younger Marguerite) was widowed in Armenia, she remarried Mardiros Malkonian and the couple immigrated to America and settled in Albany, New York. Marguerite and Mardiros had one child, Edward (born 1914). Ed was educated in the Albany area and earned a degree in Pharmacology. He successfully transformed his father's small candy store in the Troy, New York area into the Green Cross Pharmacy. Many years later Richard Sarajian, first born to Dick and Arax, would spend many weekends with Eddie and his wife Ruth while he was attending Albany Law School.

Continuing on with Yeghishe's family in Arabgir, Yeznik Catchouny was closest in age to Yeghishe. We believe he was two or three years older than Yeghishe. At the start of the Genocide when the Turks exiled Der Hoosig to Constantinople from Arabgir (we will discuss this event later in depth), all four sons accompanied him. Only Marguerite remained in Arabgir. Yeznik's life paralleled Yeghishe in many aspects. He attended law school with Yeghishe, and later he fought alongside his brother in Antranik's volunteer army. Yeznik has been described as being instrumental in developing the Homenitmen movement and an early force in the AGAU, (Armenian General Athletic Union). We know he immigrated to Persia (Iran) after the war and we have no knowledge of him ever marrying. In Persia, Yeznik was reported to work in the food industry as a butcher or a sausage maker.

Chapter 26

Yeghishe's Parents: Der Hoosig and Narthouhi Hazarian

Hagop Hazarian, a bright and pious young man, was about twenty-five years old when he married Nartouhi Shaboyan. Within a decade Hagop was the father of two boys and a girl and he made a momentous life-changing decision. Hagop, at the age of almost thirty-five found the calling to become a priest. So Baron Hagop became Der Hoosig and was so ordained in 1886. Der Hoosig ("Father Luke") was assigned to the parish of St. Illuminator's in the Shahroz district of Arabgir by Archbishop Yeznik Apahuni. (Note of interest- the Der Hayr had three children when he entered the clergy. His next child was born just about the time Hagop took his vows and became Der Hoosig. The name he chose for his new born son was Yeznik, the name of his Prelate.)

There were four churches in Arabgir. The largest or Mother church was Church of the Holy Mother of God. Besides Der Hayr's own parish of St. Illuminators, the other two churches were St. Hagop and St. Kevork. Around 1890, Der Hoosig now a father of four boys and a girl, was appointed Locum Tenens in his district by the Prelate. He was also assigned to serve as a member of the Religious and Executive Council of Arabgir by His Grace Archbishop Apahuni.

The Der Hayr's appointment was a significant honor for a priest of such limited experience. He served in that position until the dark days of the Ottoman savagery of 1895. It was shortly after the untimely death of the Yeretzgin (his wife Nartouhi) when the Der Hayr was confronted with the horrors of the '95 massacres. In Arabgir (as well as throughout Anatolia) the Turks committed a continuous vendetta of shameless and bloody slaughter. Countless thousands were butchered regardless of age or sex. The killing fields were everywhere, in the homes, churches, village streets and town squares. Bodies littered the landscape.

The Red Sultan, Abdul Hamid, (a far cry from the "Shadow of Allah on Earth") reveled in his decade of bloodletting. The Hamidian Calvary with swords drawn ran rough-shod through virtually every Armenian village. The "Gavoors" needed these periodic lessons by their Islamic Guardians. One day, late in 1895, Der Hoosig was dragged before the local Turkish officials. The "politicians" now sought some justification for the carnage. They thrust an official Ottoman document before the priest which Der Hoosig was "required" to sign. The paper admitted knowledge and complicity by all the Armenians of Arabgir to commit treason against the Empire. The Turks had brazenly shifted the responsibility of the wanton killings back upon their victims. They accused those they murdered as zealots of revolution, bent on treachery and sedition. "They brought death upon themselves," the Turkish town officials shouted. But the dead and dying, the innocent children, the women and aged attested to the true mantle of guilt.

Of course, the Der Hayr refused to be part of such an outlandish admission. Agreeing to, or giving any credence to this outrageous fabrication would be a grievous betrayal to all that the Priest held precious and sacred. It would defame his name, his family, his people, his church, his faith and his very God. He would gladly face death rather than put his mark on such a vile untruth. And so, face death he did. The Turkish court determined that "Der Hoosig Kahana Hazarian was an educated clergyman, Locum Tenens in his community, and had refused to admit to, and sign his name to an official document of responsibility. Therefore Der Hoosig was guilty of an act of treason against the Sultan." For this crime he was sentenced to imprisonment in Kharpet, and then, at a time to be determined, to be hung by the neck until dead.

So this simple but uncommon act of courage and devotion to his people would elevate Der Hoosig from priestly hero to an Arabgir legend. From that day forward the name Hazarian was changed, transformed and honored to Catchouny – "The Brave One," by all who knew him. Der Hoosig's fearless stand against the Turkish Court would cost him dearly. He was jailed in the prison of Kharpet as decreed and held there for about two years awaiting the execution of his sentence (in more than one sense).

Fortunately for Der Hoosig, "strong protestation" against the death verdict was sent to the Government Court in Kharpet from what is described as "the highest center" in Constantinople (could it have been the Armenian Patriarch?). The death sentence was eventually commuted and the Priest was saved from the gallows of Kharpet prison. Instead, Der Hoosig was banished from his home and church and sent to Constantinople to serve out his exile under the surveillance of the Armenian Patriarch of Constantinople. His sons were permitted to accompany him, but his daughter Marguerite remained in Arabgir.

Chapter 27

April 24, 1915- The Young Turks Implement their Plan to Destroy the Armenian Race

After the declaration of the new Constitution in the National Election, Der Hoosig was granted new freedoms. He was elected a delegate and a member of the Religious Council of Constantinople and he participated successfully in two councils. He was also appointed to serve on the Church Councils of Soorp Garabed Churches in Yeny-Capoo and Esgundar. As a dedicated and highly qualified Priest, he was vigorously involved in national clerical affairs until the demise of the Hamidian era.

Der Catchouny's activism caught the demonic eye of Interior Minister Talaat and on the eve of April 24, 1915, Der Hoosig was among the first Armenian religious, political, social, and industrial leaders of Constantinople who were arrested, interned

215

and forced to endure the indignities of Turkish prisons. The Turks had systematically amputated the muscle from the Armenian community by conscripting all the Armenian youth to serve in the military. This mandatory "draft" served the Turkish needs in two ways. It provided the army a labor force for the most servile martial duties imaginable. Secondly, it excised the young and strong from the restless Armenian communities. The conscripts were fully controlled, confined and restricted. All non-Moslems were denied the right to bear any arms, swords or knives. When the "hammer struck" the Armenian youth fell, unable to fight or defend themselves and those they left behind.

In Constantinople Der Hoosig Catchouny along with thousands of the nation's finest minds and stalwart contributors were labeled and condemned as traitors. Their only crime was THEY WERE ARMENIAN. This lawless Ottoman justice swept up and disposed of the most influential and powerful Armenians in Bolis. The "blitz" was carefully aimed to snuff out the brightest lights and extinguish the rekindled flame of Armenian nationalism. The remainder of the Armenian race was to flicker away, quietly expiring along the fiery pathways to perdition. The scorching deserts of Syria and Persia awaited. The searing sands would serve as the prearranged crematoriums for the survivors of the exile marches.

This then was their plan! This was the terrible Turkish tactic to achieve a final solution regarding Armenians. Blanched bones buried in desert caves and the remains of decomposing roadside corpses could never be honored or glorified. No martyrs here, only waste. But instead, even in death these humiliated, mutilated vestiges bequeathed their desecrated and unrecognizable remains as a final offering. It proved to be the evidence that shocked the world. It is now called GENOCIDE!!! This very word was assigned to describe the Armenian Tragedy!

Starting on the night of April 23, 1915, the armies of "Young Turk" and local gendarme death squads, struck quickly with precise and lethal results. Whatever little muscle the Armenians possessed, had been neutralized within the walls of military camps and compounds. In Constantinople, the Turks assaulted the head of their internal foe, the mind and brains of the Armenian intelligentsia. What an ingenious plan. Paralyze the muscle and then cut off the head. Then, simply throw the "riff-raff" that remains into the dessert. Ergo – no more Armenians, no more Armenians, no more Armenians!

Using available historic census figures, a comparison of the Armenian population in Ottoman Turkey in the early 1900's (approximately three million), to present day figures (approximately 50,000- of which 49,000 reside in the metropolitan Istanbul area), yields a remarkable statistic. In the past 100 years the population of Armenians in the ancient Armenian homeland has diminished by almost 98 ½ %. Most of losses occurred in the first twenty five years of the 20th Century. The conclusion being – Abdul Hamid, Talaat Pasha and his Young Turk cohorts and Ataturk can claim almost complete success in carrying out their planned defoliation of the Armenian Flower and its' seed from its native soil.

Chapter 28

Der Hoosig's Remarkable Exile

The remarkable end story of Der Hoosig's final exile and expiration, his year-long personal journey into the "Valley of the Shadow of Death" was documented on, of all places, a single oval prayer bead. This smooth tawny stone bore the inscription of his name (carved Kachuni). I believe it was the fourth bead on a string that indexed the names and fate of one hundred and three victims of this macabre march out of Constantinople. These were the exiles to Changri. (Changri is the name of a Turkish village and a depot of death).

The names of the banished prisoners were skillfully crafted onto the beads by fellow captive Vardres Atamasian. Who could have imagined that these carved names of one hundred and three martyrs emblazoned upon beads of prayer would conserve and perpetuate their identities. In essence, those tiny stones would somehow serve as substitute (and formidable) grave-markers. A sacrament that few, if any, death marchers could claim. But at least one hundred and three souls would have their names remembered upon these miniature prayer beads, these proxy gravestones. The bodies of the exiles would perish and vanish but the inscribed stones survived and served as their final testaments.

The following is an eye-witness description of the fate of Der Hoosig and the rest of this group of intellectuals, clergy, politicians and leaders that was rounded up by the Turks on April 24, 1915.

Three days after his (Der Hoosig's) arrest the Der Hayr was deported by boat, and then by train to the city of Enburg. From Enburg the deportees were culled into smaller groups of one hundred or less. From Enburg they were assigned to horse-drawn carriages. Each carriage held five or six exiles. Der Hoosig's wagon held four other clergymen. Three were Vartabeds or celibate priests and one other was a Der Hayr or non-celibate clergyman.[28]

A.   Der Hoosig's Fellow Exile: Gomidas Vartabed

When I read the names of Der Hoosig's co-prisoners, one name caught my eye. Besides Der Hayr Vartan, the Vartabeds were Hayr Krikoris, Hayr

Hovnan and finally Gomidas Vartabed. The time and place seemed right to me. Was this "Gomidas" the same renowned Armenian composer? Most Armenians will at least recognize the name of Gomidas Vartabed. This unassuming, almost shy cleric had his hands and heart in perfect harmony with the very soul of Armenian music. He has been depicted as a legend among legends and as a true Armenian treasure, a national saint. Further, he has been characterized as the savior and conserver of Armenian folk music and the founder of the Armenian classical theme. When the remains of Gomidas were returned to Armenia and were buried in the shadow of Ararat, the great Armenian poet Avedis Isahakian wrote, "You are now in the bosom of the genuine soil of your motherland. The loving song of the aromatic plain of Ararat is looming about you as your own songs are ripening upon you. Rest in peace dear Gomidas, divine Gomidas."

Astonished as I was to discover this link between Hoosig Kahana and Gomidas Vartabed I needed to establish some further proof of identity. Was this the Gomidas Vartabed? Using my best source, I called my brother-in-law Krikor Pidedjian. Krikor is a renowned musicologist, a composer and arranger of both folk and liturgical music. Besides, he has been an enthusiastic advocate of Gomidas and has lectured on the life and accomplishments of the venerable Vartabed. In fact, I myself photographed Krikor (and he was in tears) as he stood upon the very same stage in Constantinople where Gomidas lectured his young students a century earlier. I don't think I ever saw Krikor look so shaken, thrilled and overwhelmed. Now almost nine years later when I explained my quandary to Krikor, he carefully questioned my sources of information. When he heard that Der Hoosig's caravan was destined for Changhri – BAM!!! This is the place and time. It was here that the semi-conscious, beaten and battered Gomidas (now forty-six years old) was traced and then recalled by the Turks to Constantinople. According to Krikor Pidedjian, the enormously talented Gomidas survived his exile destiny to Der Zor (in Syria) due to the intervention of Ambassador Morgenthau and a Prince of the Ottoman Royal Family. Gomidas' name and his musical genius were well known by Morgenthau and the Ottoman Prince had a personal relationship with the Vartabed. His two daughters had been students of Gomidas and had idolized their teacher.

But the quest to return Gomidas to safety was too late. While the hungry and thirsty Vartabed waited his turn to receive a cup full of water, a brutal gendarme struck the gentle clergyman a shattering blow to the head with a rifle butt. This "special" act of savagery was reserved for "cloaked and hooded celibate priests" and was enthusiastically exercised. Gomidas never fully recovered. When he was returned to Constantinople, Gomidas was immediately hospitalized. As he lay hapless, helpless and almost hopeless in "Bolis" both his senses and sensibilities remained permanently scrambled.

After war's end, sometime in 1919, Gomidas Vartabed was transferred to a hospital in Paris. The priest spent the rest of his life in an asylum and finally found his heavenly peace in 1935. He was sixty-six years old, almost the exact age of his co-prisoner Der Hoosig when he perished nineteen years earlier. From Paris the remains of Gomidas Vartabed were requested and sent to Armenia. But his true remains, his music, will live on forever in the hearts and on the lips of his beloved Armenian people.

B. Der Hoosig in Hamman

Back in Changhri after the unexpected recall of Gomidas Vartabed, the exiles tattered and hungry were secured and encamped. They remained in Changhri for some time. When the journey resumed on its southward trek (to the deserts of Syria), the caravan eventually passed a village called Hammam. For some unexplained and unknown reason, Der Hoosig was permitted to leave the group, and he settled down alone in a tiny tent on the edge of this remote Islamic village. Hammam was a small Arab enclave, some four or five villages from the final destination of Der Zor. Der Zor was the end of the trail- the finish- the final mile for untold countless thousands. Der Zor was the unsanctified catch-basin destined to cradle the tangle and scramble of skeletal debris in the pit-oven of the Syrian inferno. This was the gravesite without gravestones or markers. It was the burial place desecrated rather than consecrated by man unto his brother. Sadly it was not a final resting place but a final wasting place. It was the Turks "deliverance" to Armenians.

Der Hoosig was spared the death grottos of Der Zor and was given considerable freedom by Hammam's Arab residents. He lived out his last days in his tiny tent. There is some evidence that Der Hoosig continued to be of service to God in Hammam. Stories of the weakened Priest celebrating "Badarak," (Mass), for the few scattered Armenian refugees in the area have emerged from this isolated Arab village. Sometime in 1916 the aged "Priest Kachuni" succumbed to want, disease and despair. He was about sixty-five years old. The Kahana's troubled frame was no longer able to shoulder the constant suffering of mind and body, but never of soul and spirit. His earthly remains mingle with the sands of Hammam, but his Heavenly remains rest with our Lord and our God.

C. The Beads of Changri

As discussed above, Der Hoosig's participation in the caravan of intellectuals, clerics and others was documented on the so-called Beads of Changri. This string of beads simply and unceremoniously foretold the death of those thereon inscribed. The first name was Gomidas. Another name, Grigor Pilakian, who escaped the prophecy of the beads and later wrote

"Armenian Golgotha" which helps explain the meaning of these cryptic crystals. This book along with some extensive research and intensive investigation helped to document the fate of each exile whose name was so inscribed.

One day a few years ago, Surpazan Mesrop explored the pages of a small paperback journal. Archbishop Ashjian could often be found searching for answers in obscure volumes that hid in dusty archives which contained Armenian literature. The Archbishop's discerning eye brightened as it captured names, facts and events he knew to be of significant importance to the family of one of his closest friends and parishioners, the family of Dick Sarajian.

The Archbishop was able to purchase one of the few remaining copies of this little book and gifted it to the heirs of Der Hoosig Kahana Catchouny and Yeghishe Catchouny. Of course this is the book which reveals the amazing story of "The Relic of the Prayer Beads."

Eventually I entrusted that very copy to my own brother-in-law as he departed for Yerevan in the fall of 2006. I had hoped that Krikor Pidedjian, with his thirst for Armenian artifacts and his fund of contacts of Yerevantsi scholars would be able to find, identify, photograph and perhaps even hold the beads. I knew Krikor would be drawn to "bead number one," bearing the name of Gomidas. Of no lesser interest to the Catchouny ancestors was the tiny amulet inscribed with Catchouny name. Krikor returned to America unable to fulfill his quest in 2006 and 2007.

However, in 2008, Krikor accomplished his mission. Krikor, together with an Armenian friend named Alexan and Alexan's mother (a close friend of the Director of a Yerevan museum), and Krikor's wife Berjouhi, visited the Armenian National Historic Museum in Yerevan. Krikor met with the Director of the museum who announced that the beads were being prepared for their inaugural showing as part of a new Genocide wing at the museum. The Director mentioned that if it were not for her relationship with Alexan's mother, she would not been inclined to this "pre-inaugural" viewing of the beads. The group was escorted into the new wing of the museum and to the area where the Beads of Changri were displayed.

Krikor took many photographs of the deep red string of beads which memorialized the names of the exiles of Changri. Displayed with the beads was a document which identified the 103 engraved names on the 99 tiny, fingernail-sized amulets. The first name on the beads was, of course, Gomidas Vartabed. The fourth name was Kahana Kachuni.

Krikor was allowed to remove the beads from the case and he gently embraced these tokens of sacrifice in his trembling hands. The beads were light in weight, likely composed of an item of vegetable property such as a bean or a nut. They seemed too light to be made of stone or metal. The beads were similar to each other, symmetrical and smooth to the touch. Their reddish-brown hue appeared to glow as if to illuminate the names of the martyrs. The delicate Armenian script is tiny, so skillfully engraved that one would need the use of a jeweler's loop or engraver's glass to identify each meticulous carving.

The Beads of Changri and their story will be on permanent display in the genocide wing of the Armenian National Historic Museum in Yerevan, Armenia. I owe my heartfelt appreciation to Krikor Pidedjian who's dogged determination to uncover and view these miniature remembrances has helped to verify and historically corroborate Der Catchouny's participation in the stirring tale of the Beads of Changri.

In 1915 "The Monstrous Mother of Murders" was intended not only to kill but to denigrate and degrade the Armenian spirit. The Turkish resolve was directed not only to erase the nation of Armenians but to historically suffocate all evidence of their very existence. Few if any Genocide victims were memorialized in graves, burial sites or even by simple markers in Turkey. Millions of Turkey's own citizens will never be found, lost forever. There are a scarce scattering of Armenian gravestones and vestiges of "bone yards" but weathered dust particles were the only end product for most of the slain. Fortunately in the rare case of Der Hoosig, the evidence and fate of his existence lies not with his withered bones in a lonely Arab outpost. His remains have been swept among the sands with the wind, but not his epithet, not his memory. A caring compatriot etched his name in a bead and so, his very being was immortalized.

Chapter 29

Yeghishe and Yeznik Finish Law School

I am afraid that little is known of the lives of the Catchouny (Hazarian) children after the imprisonment of Der Hayr in Kharpet. As mentioned, there is some indication that the boys were allowed to join Der Hoosig in his exile to Constantinople in 1896 or 1897. We do know that both Yeznik and Yeghishe, the two youngest, were gifted students and very active in athletics.

Yeznik and Yeghishe participated with much skill and enthusiasm in the national sport of soccer. Their love of the game would never abate. Engaging at all age levels of the sport would be a happy and meaningful diversion for both far into their adulthood. Yeznik in Iran and Yeghishe in America still competed with gusto far from the football fields of Turkey.

As the two brothers matured they both exhibited quick and clever intellects. From secondary school they each qualified for the university, but I am unsure if they received academic scholarships or obtained financial aid from the Patriarchy. In 1914 the brothers Catchouny together graduated from Law School at the University of Constantinople.

While studying for his degree in law, one of Yeghishe's closest classmates was Zaven Gorgodian. Zaven was a bit older than Yeghishe and he had traveled across the country to fulfill his own dream of becoming a barrister. Together, Yeghishe and Zaven made exciting plans for the future. They were determined to become law partners. Zaven came from a vibrant and flourishing city called Van. Van was located almost beneath the shadow of Mt. Ararat in the far eastern provinces. Both Zaven and Yeghishe were convinced that Van would offer more opportunities to succeed in a new law practice. Of course, Arabgir, Yeghishe's native village, would be less than politically hospitable to a Catchouny. Constantinople was certainly big, bustling and busy. The large city was enticing and offered much, but it was a difficult place to compete, especially for two young Armenian lawyers. Remember, in 1914 "Bolis," was a city ruled ruthlessly by the Young Turks and under wartime sanctions. The Armenian condition with the new government had deteriorated since the start of World War I. The fragile truce and kinship of mutual trust, which seemed to develop after the fall of the Ottoman Empire and the Sultan was eroding. The Young Turks were taking turns in manipulating the Armenian leaders in a game of "Good Guy-Bad Guy." Talaat was feared and avoided. Enver seemed sympathetic and Djemal played both roles. The Armenian populace no longer felt ignored. Now they were uneasy, uncomfortable and even felt unwelcome.

Considering the state of the country, most Armenians felt outright threatened. Yeghishe and Zaven agreed. Bolis was much too unstable, too turbulent, and too stormy, they would head east.

Van had many advantages. First of all it was, geographically a neighbor of Russia. Remember, this was Czarist and Christian Russia, as opposed to Islamic Turkey. Russia was always thought of as a friend to the Armenians and a territorial and religious adversary to Islamic Turkey. Besides, Van offered an expanding community with a burgeoning economy. The population of Van was now in excess of 100,000, with the Armenians in the majority. Even of more significance, the Armenians held vital political positions in Van and were in control of much of the city's functions and services. Such a site seemed an ideal starting point for the two ambitious young attorneys, war or no war.

Chapter 30

Van and Aghtamar: A Historical and Personal Look

A. The City of Van

Van had developed into a surprisingly sophisticated city of the Middle East. It had evolved from the ancient city (Tahhupixa-Priori, in the tenth century, BC [29]) to a modern cosmopolitan gem. Adding to its urbane, even worldly "mini-city" reputation, Van was a visual delight. The walled city was built just a stone's throw from the sparkling waters of Lake Van. Its scenic splendor was further enhanced by a circular rim of ragged snow-peaked mountains.

If the landscape of Van was "upscale" so were its citizens. The Vanetzsis were somehow able to alter and remodel their customs and their costumes

232

from the Eastern Anatolian to the western mode of the Europeans. Dresses and suits were not only commonplace, they were every place. Ottoman and Kurdish garb were the exception in the city.

Van was attractive, active, big and sprawling. The Old City strained at its walls. At the turn of the century Van consisted of more than 5000 congested homes and businesses. The streets were cobble-stoned, narrow and featured a kaleidoscope of buildings that varied from small and simple to affluent and opulent. Abruptly attractive homesteads would adjoin wallowing habitats in disrepair. The homes almost reflected the cultural and ethnic background of their occupants. This central area of "Old Van" encompassed almost twenty-five square kilometers. Within this locale Van had committed its seven churches, (some buildings surprisingly constructed of wood), and six mosques. Of course the city reveled in its large and constantly active bazaar region. This was the central point, the hub of the city's economic dynamics. Every Middle Eastern metropolis, large or small, was dependent on this collection depot for foods, goods and general trade. Van took pride in its expansive mix of Arab, Kurdish, Turkish, Armenian, Russian and European commerce.

The overcrowded Old City gave rise to the inexorable urban spread of Van. Outside the ancient walls sprouted forth the new and desirable "Garden District." Tall stately Poplar trees encircled this prosperous sector. Many inhabitants of the "district" recall that the entire site was a fertile orchard of apple, peach, pomegranate and other fruit trees. Vanetzsis still boast that the rich earth provided an over abundance of giant melons and cucumbers. Five churches and five mosques graced the wondrous expanse of the "Garden District".

This blossoming new Van, together with the Old City boasted a total of eighteen schools, eleven of which were Armenian and seven Turkish. Most schools were public, but a few private institutions did exist. The private schools were considered "elite" and the children of the wealthy competed for admittance and a more comprehensive learning experience. Among most Vanities a thorough education was considered mandatory, a priority for both boys and girls.

After the turn of the century the international community discovered Van. Foreign representatives found this new Van to be an attractive and more desirable alternative to the unavoidable squalor of the large Turkish cities. In the early 1900's there were three consulates established in the Garden District: British, Russian and Persian. In addition the Italian and Austrian embassies had posted Consul Agents for diplomatic service. A few other countries were considering moving their foreign offices to Van. Van's idyllic setting, together with the relatively high standards of its populace made Van sparkle as a haven in the wilderness.

Van was not overlooked by the "religious reformers" as well. The American Board of Protestant Churches had founded a significantly powerful mission within the city. The Catholic Church, not to be outdone, was also active in its missionary calling, as well as its ever present quest in garnering converts within its folds. The Dominican Brotherhood was the Vatican's representative in Van.

The Old City had historically sprawled lake ward from its imposing three hundred foot high barrier cliff and the ancient fortifications which stood atop its crest. This landmark, "The Citadel" was the signature identity of Van. The origin of the fort (or "pert" in Armenian) dates back to the Uratian Period, about 7 B.C. The Ottomans rebuilt and reinforced the rock and stone battlements after they swarmed into Anatolia in the sixteenth century.

When I visited the plains of Van in June of 1998, I instinctively sensed that our group stood as one, aghast, stunned and appalled at what we saw. We remained silent for awhile, self-absorbing and reexamining the contrasting emotions that welled within us. I became aware of the eerie peacefulness of Van's pastoral landscape. A brilliant blue Anatolian sky washed the scene in a wondrous glow. But we weren't in awe; we were dumbstruck and astounded by the totality of destruction throughout the region. There were no homes, or semblance of homes. No rock piles of ruins. Not even a remote resemblance of the crowded urban center that once was. Even the outline or geometry of foundations, of streets and avenues were not recognizable. For some reason the crumbling remnants of three churches punctuated this ghostly wasteland. Those barely discernible ruins lay in isolated, stony heaps sharing the forsaken landscape with two intact but abandoned mosques. There was nothing else. These spiritual monuments, or rather, religious specters, gave silent testimony to the blood bath which had wasted Van. It was as if a mindful God (Allah) would not let us ever forget.

What remains of the once guardian City Wall of Van was in many places a blistered mound of rocky rubble, only three or four feet high. Its protective shield was no longer necessary. With the help of Professors Cowe and Hewsen and Archbishop Mesrop Ashjian we were able to identify one of the four original entry portals into the Old City. The "ground" underfoot and throughout the city appeared to be frozen in motion, like the still photo of ocean waves. What we saw is what had evolved after eighty years of blight and erosion. The human scavengers (bands of Kurds and Turks) had picked the city clean, and left the rest to natures' winds, sun and storms. What remained were mounds, hillock, valleys and depressions. Scant pieces of tile, glass, pottery and foundation stones were scattered about aimlessly. The grave like elevations of soil were a result of the heaving firmament of a once great city. Now silenced, sullen and suffocated by a century's deposit of its own dust and grime heaped upon itself. It remains desolate, like a forsaken orphan, cast aside and forgotten.

When Herand Markarian, the noted Armenian-American historian visited his ancestral home of Van in 1997, he was devastated and overwhelmed. Markarian collapsed on the soil of his forefathers and openly wept at the calamity exposed before him. He was well aware of what to expect, but still was unable to fathom the trauma and transformation. From what was to what is too sorrowful to grasp.

I know I will never forget both the pleasure and the pain I derived from experiencing the total conditions of what was Van. It was all here to see, the beauty and the battered. Nor will neither I, nor others forget the soulful reflections of Archbishop Ashjian as he stood amidst the rock pile of ruins of Soorp Nishan Church. He was in shocked mourning, consumed with anguish. In a trembling, crackling and throaty voice that was so unique to him, he soliloquized, "if only this hallowed ground could reveal its secrets to us. Who knows, perhaps someday, some way, the tragedy of Van will be known to all?" I remember the moment well, for I videotaped His Eminence in his reverie. Above all, I remember Mesrop Ashjian as a son of Armenia, brimming with passion and emotion. Predictably when this pious Priest was confronted with such moments of exquisite sensitivity, he would express himself physically as well as emotionally. He bowed his head as if in prayer, and trembling, a solitary sob escaped his lips and a lonely tear drained from our loving Prelate's eye. A tear he shed for all Vanetzsis, for all Armenians.

As our Prelate wept he was in communion with all of us who crave and search for the truth. But perhaps, (in truth), we may be better off in the silent solemnity of the long buried past. Standing tall in the bright sunlight, his feet planted firmly atop the wild grasses of the Van plains, the Archbishop fulfilled our request for a Hoki Hankist in the names of Yeghishe and Satenig Catchouny and their families as well as all the victims and survivors of Van. Peace of mind and solace of heart are not always easily found through tears, but still again, Surpazan's prayers comforted our aches.

No description of Van could be complete without a visit to the Island of Aghtamar and the Church of the Holy Cross. Aghtamar Island is located a few miles off the southeastern shore of Lake Van. The size of the lake itself is quite impressive. It is approximately one hundred miles long and sixty miles wide in its maximum dimensions. The lake lies in an East-West configuration in East Central Anatolia. Its maximum depth approaches two thousand feet. It is an alpine body of water at an altitude of about one mile. The lake is fed by a system of mountain streams and has no natural outlet. The degree of water loss is almost totally dependent upon evaporation. Flooding of shoreline villages, such as Khorkom, the birthplace of the celebrated Armenian artist Ashville Gorky, are quite common.

The color of the lake is a striking blue-green azure. The pH chemistry of the lake is highly alkaline due to the abundant lakebed deposits of borax. Prolonged exposure to lake water while bathing or swimming can prove to be irritating to the eyes and skin. However, washing clothes in lake water is a boon due to the cleansing properties of borax.

B. The Island of Aghtamar

The craggy island of Aghtamar is a short boat ride from the southern shore of the lake. The island is tiny, picturesque, irregular but generally triangular in shape. It covers about a quarter of a square mile of dry land. The island peaks to a maximum elevation of two hundred sixty two feet above the splash of the brilliant blue waters.

Aghtamar was selected by Armenian King Gagik Artsruni in 915 AD as an ideal naturally-protected site for his lavish palace, a magnificent church, a monastery and a compact village consisting of an estimated five hundred families.[30] The village would of course shelter the laborers who would spend years constructing the palace and church. Only scant fragments of the village are recoverable today. All traces of the Palace are gone and even present day historians have difficulty in describing the palatial structure. Some experts believe that the Palace was located just south and almost abutting the Church. It was believed to be an astounding edifice, which was topped by a magnificent eighty-foot dome. The dome, an architectural marvel in itself, rose high above a vaulted and gilded throne room. This was a throne room of stunning opulence. The walls of the Palace were profusely decorated with the finest frescoes and paintings available. The scenes depicted within the interior are believed to be of a similar motif portrayed by the stone carvings, which embellish the outside walls of the Church. Historians rationalize that the village was built first and then the Palace.

The construction of the Church of the Holy Cross began in 915 A.D. and was completed by 921 A.D., an amazing architectural and engineering accomplishment. The Artsruni dynasty was a major player in the burgeoning growth of Christianity in the Tenth Century. Armenian Kings and Princes throughout the expanse of Armenia spared neither cost nor effort in the exultation and glorification of the faith.

In Aghtamar, Gagik Artsruni's royal ambitions soared much higher than his lofty Palace dome. Artsruni's dreams envisioned the establishment of a Catholicate on Aghtamar to "sanctify" his Kingly efforts and to secure his power base. But his heirs and subjects would have to wait for two more centuries before his desires became realities. Finally in the year 1116 A.D. and for the following three centuries the Princes of Artsruni assumed and controlled the exalted throne of the Catholicos of Aghtamar. During this timeframe a serious schism estranged the Catholicates of Aghtamar and Etchmiadzin. The "play" for supremacy between the two Armenian religious titans and their regal support base was extinguished when Ottoman expansionism consumed the Christian middle and near east territories. With his decline of power and influence, the Catholicos of Aghtamar, in the sixteenth century, abandoned all hope of being ordained the "Hairabed" or "Chief" or "Head Catholicos."

Centuries later, after the reign of Catholicos Katchadour (1864-1895), Aghtamar's prestige declined dramatically. A significant factor was the election of a dynamic abbot from a nearby Van monastery, Varakavank, who was destined to glorify the Armenian Nation from Etchmiadzin. "Khrimian Hairik" of Van was ordained Catholicos of all Armenians in Etchmiadzin. Hence ended the dispute of two Kingdoms and two Catholic. For the next twenty years, the Church of the Holy Cross on Aghtamar Island was allowed to "remain dormant." It almost appeared as if "Holy Cross" at Aghtamar was now required to pay penance for years of schism with Etchmiadzin. The Palace of Aghtamar and the village that built it had disappeared centuries earlier.

Then in 1915, the Turks overran and destroyed the monastery, killed the resident monks and looted the church. It appeared as if the final chapter of the Glory of Aghtamar had been written, and once again it was the "bloodied Sword of Crescent" that punctuated the period.

When I visited the magical island of Aghtamar and the Church of the Holy Cross, I recall how much our group anticipated this precious moment. How well I remember standing within the Church, upon shards of fractured marble and rocky rubble. As Pilgrims we perched upon ruins of the past one hundred years. Still once again we stood amongst mans' abuses and nature's ceaseless ravages. I thought "this was once polished marble and granite and was graced by the slippered feet of Kings and Princes, of Hairabeds and unending pious streams of devout Armenian Christians." I felt dwarfed, somehow diminished by the enormity of the experience; of the opportunity to be touched by 1000 years of glorious and turbulent history.

Our entire group of twenty gathered reverently about Surpazan Mesrop, both humbled and thrilled by the spell and aura of this special, sacred place. I kept thinking, "Am I really here?" and I answered "Yes I am!" I am really standing in the hallowed sanctuary of both a consecrated Temple and an Armenian architectural jewel. I am shielded by the graceful dome of the Church of the Holy Cross which has sheltered and looked down upon centuries of

Armenian History. I believe each of us fed off the energy generated by our neighbor, our fellow pilgrim. The mood we shared spiritually seemed to fuse us into one, one heart, one mind, and one spirit. I don't believe any of us could be more Armenian than at that moment within the Holy Tabernacle of Aghtamar. I fervently hope these words and emotions will encourage some readers to explore the possibility of sharing such a moment of pure joy on Aghtamar Island sometime in the future.

Although the views and vistas surrounding the Church of the Holy Cross are breathtaking and inspiring, I could not help but feel saddened and depressed cringing at yet another Armenian Church denigrated and defaced. It is with abject disrespect that the government of Turkey, and yes, even the faith of Islam, has permitted these Christian monuments to God to languish and deteriorate. The uncaring hand of the host and keeper of the nation's relics is guilty of profane neglect. The one hundred years of weathering and erosion bereft of even primitive protection and rudimentary restoration is unforgivable. The transformation of a church into mosque (a recurring theme in Turkey) is sacrilegious. The transition from Church to museum is no less scandalous.

Of course the island of Aghtamar and the Church of the Holy Cross only "survives" in the guardianship, the trust of the Turks. I will never concede to recognize the ownership of Soorp Khatch to the Turk. What has been dedicated to God is forever God's. I know that recent efforts have been made to "clean up" and even reinforce the Church. The rededication of the Church of the Holy Cross into a secular "Turkish" museum has only further denigrated the Armenian Faith and Heritage. The Turkish government has attempted to alter a "House of God" into "Tourist Trade Trappings." SHAME!! SHAME!! SHAME!!! Perhaps Aghtamar will continue to survive but a thousand other "Aghtamars" are naught but rubble. Even more sadly, most lie atop the unmarked graves of their martyred parishioners.

For some time now the Turkish Tourist Board has maintained a ferry service to the island. The boat ride is short and stunningly scenic. After docking there it is a fifteen to twenty minute gentle pathway climb to the Church. On our pilgrimage there were dozens of local Kurdish picnickers visiting Aghtamar and most would stay the day. One of my more memorable moments on Aghtamar, once again, involved Archbishop Mesrop. As we filed slowly into the Church, led by Surpazan, Berjouhi Pidedjian (my wife's sister) sang the Sanctus (Soorp) from the Armenian Badarak (Mass). I could not help but question when the last time was when such a beautiful voice echoed in this holy place? The Archbishop celebrated a Memorial Service that somehow seemed a bit more "evoking" than the many we had attended during our long journey.

After the service, the Archbishop called our attention to an eighteen year old girl he met an hour earlier on the ferry dock. This young lady saw and recognized Surpazan after she disembarked returning from Aghtamar. The teenager was traveling with a non-Armenian girlfriend and they were touring the interior "alone" on a journey similar to our own. The Armenian girl was the daughter of a prominent Philadelphia physician. Both she and her family were long time friends of the Prelate. As Archbishop Ashjian spun his "homily" of this unexpected but happy meeting, a beam of light from a dome window above found and spotlighted the Surpazan. The light bathed his back and shoulders and haloed his head. I don't believe he even noticed it, but Hrair "Hawk" Katcherian, the gifted Canadian-Armenian photographer (a member of our group,) grasped the moment and took the shot. In his album of exquisite photographic memoirs, that one, touched by the "Spirit," with Surpazan in the "glow," was to me, graphic proof of our pilgrimage. In the stony silence of the church His Eminence spoke, softly, almost in a whisper as upon the altar, prayfully. His gripping words, his message, touched and thrilled us all. His final sentence still rings in my heart.

"As long as young Armenians, like this teenager from Philadelphia, come to honor and pray in this place, it will always be ours!"

Once again, if you can, come visit and pray in Aghtamar. If unable, I heartily recommend a stunningly beautiful book titled "Aghtamar and the Church of the Holy Cross 915-921." It was published by the Alex Manoogian Cultural Fund of the A.G.B.U. It is a spectacular pictorial history of Aghtamar.

One final note about Aghtamar Island. It is a tale concerning our great national hero, Antranik Ozanian. There are countless stories, songs and poems celebrating the feats of Orator (Brave) Antranik. This one tells of the times the General used the island as a refuge, a hideout, a sanctuary from his Turkish pursuers. On this one occasion Antranik's foes discovered his lair. They flooded the area with troops and surrounded the island with patrol boats. The shrewd and elusive freedom fighter was up to the task. Antranik stealthily slipped away in the dark of a moonless night. The legend has it that he braved the icy waters of Lake Van and swam the four or five miles to a secluded beach on the far shore. The story is chilling enough, but many insist that Antranik made his astounding escape entirely underwater and atop his great white stallion!

Chapter 31

Yeghishe in Van

The year was 1914 and Yeghishe Catchouny, now almost twenty-five years old, together with his friend Zaven Gorgodian opened a law office in the "old city" of Van. We believe that that the two young attorneys lived in the Gorgodian home. The Gorgodian family compound in the elite Garden District was spacious and consisted of a number of houses. Zaven's sister, Satenig, who would later become Yeghishe's wife, also lived at home with her parents, Ohaness and Hripsimeh.

Ohaness Gorgodian, Zaven and Satenig's father, was born sometime in the mid 1850's. Ohaness was a very successful dry goods merchant. He spent a great deal of time away from Van, in Turkish cities near and far. He was considered skilled and shrewd in buying, consigning and selling his wares. The comfortable lifestyle of the Gorgodian clan in the Garden District together with Satenig's remembrances concerning the high level of education afforded to all the children indicates that Ohaness was an aggressive and affluent businessman. Among his friends and neighbors Ohaness was often referred to the "mayor." Was this "title" merely a sign of respect or did the "designation" carry some political implications?

Ohaness' wife, Hripsimeh (nee Kapamajian) was probably born in the 1860's. Ohaness and Hripsimeh had 5 children. Kayane was the first born (1882?). She was married at an early age to a baker/tailor, name unknown. She had four children and lived with her family outside the Gorgodian compound, in the predominately Turkish sector of the Old City. Of course it was customary that the wife would reside with her husband's family.

Next in line was Zaven, Yeghishe's classmate and law partner. Zaven was very bright, did exceptionally well in school and was graduated with honors from the private Yerelian School in Van. After completing his education, Zaven was recruited and accepted a position as a teacher in one of Van's public Armenian Schools. A driving ambition to excel led Zaven away from Van. He crossed the country and enrolled in the Constantinople Law School where he met Yeghishe Catchouny. Zaven's birth date is sometime in the mid or late 1880's.

Philip was the younger brother and was born around 1890. He too was a well educated and gifted youngster. Philip went to a military school and served in the Turkish army as an officer. We will reveal more of Philip's adventures a bit later but for now it will suffice to say that Philip died a hero and martyr fighting for Armenian freedom in the battle of Sardarabad.

The Gorgodians had two daughters, Satenig and an adopted daughter, Vartanoush. We have meager information about Vartanoush but we do know her date of birth lies somewhere between Philip's and Satenig's.

Beside the Ohaness Gorgodian family, the compound was spacious enough to provide separate housing for Ohaness' five brothers and sisters and their families. All the Gorgodian men worked at their own trade. That is, except for the eldest brother, who was "aged" and "retired." Two of Satenig's uncles were barbers.

Yeghishe and Zaven could not have chosen a less opportune or more dangerous time to embark on their initial business venture. World War I had erupted in Europe and the political climate in Turkey was becoming increasingly ugly. Talaat Bey, most powerful of the "Young Turks" and the sinister Minister of the Interior, was frequently quoted as saying "there is only room for Turks in Turkey." Christians, and particularly Armenians were being persecuted throughout the country. Unprovoked random jailing and even public hangings of prominent Armenian businessman, civil rights crusaders and even educators became common occurrences. Local anti-Armenian pogroms spewed out of control from Smyrna to Erzurum and even to the far eastern outposts of Van. Even the sacred vestments which identified our clergy were not a guarantee against violent outrages and the cruelest abuses.

Chapter 32

Van: April 1915

It was the spring of 1915 in Van, but it wasn't the birds that were whistling, it was the barrage of shellfire that peppered the wall of the Old City. In Professor Hewson's "Historical Atlas of Armenia," the very first lithograph is a copy of a painting, the original oil of which hangs in the Topkapi Museum in Istanbul. The scene depicts Van (circa 1600A.D.) with a double wall around the city. I am unsure, but doubt that was the case in 1915.

A single wall and a handful of brave men was all the Vanities had to oppose the thrust of the Turkish army. Like the Armenians of Shabin-Karahisar, the Armenians in Van chose self-defense in the face of forced deportation. The Armenian citizens of Van had been deceived with lies, broken promises and instead, been rewarded with Turkish

251

massacres throughout the 1890's. They were now not so foolhardy as to grovel and to commit the grievous trust, (sin) of their fathers. The Armenian men of Van refused earlier orders to surrender all arms. Now they were prepared to fight and die if they must on their own soil and on their own terms.

Rumors and wild reports of massive deportations and roadside slaughter of exiles resounded everywhere and terrorized the city. The whole populace was prepared to make the Turks pay a dear price for their outrages. The Armenian warriors geared for a battle. All about the fabled Van cliff and atop the "Pert" the legions of "freedom fighters" assembled. Just north of the city a contingent of Russian troops massed and were instructed to assist the Armenians in their defense of Van. The courageous citizens of Van rallied, determined to guard each house, each school, and each church. Alice Catchouny Hagopian, Yeghishe and Satenig's eldest child, recalled her father's chilling words during one of his lectures here in America. He described the early siege of Van in these words, "The Turkish artillery continued its bombardment all day long, day after day. They would shell us during the daylight hours and their bombs blew huge holes in our Wall. Then, with the fall of darkness, we would repair the Wall all night long. Men, women, children, stone by stone, rock by rock, hand by hand!!!"

The entire Armenian world within the Anatolian Plateau was in a fiery upheaval. This was a landscape of epic proportion and of demonic genesis. "The Inferno" by Dante could be found here. Ottoman Turkey had been transformed into a countrywide cemetery. Here, in the Cradle of the Biblical Eden, the Turks exploited and terrorized their most ancient residents, the Armenians.

In every city, town, and village, deep in every cave and atop every mountain, inside every nook and outside every cranny, in and about every hiding place and along each fighting front the Armenians were fingered for death. This was not war, this was GENOCIDE, the killing of a people.

During the summer months of 1915 the siege of Van intensified. The Turks poured more troops and equipment around the city. House to house fighting fragmented and isolated the Armenian districts. Finally, lack of munitions, food and even water weakened the resolve of the defenders. When the Russian army pulled out of the fray, the outcome became apparent. The battered citizens of Van availed themselves to the single escape corridor to the north and east. Yerevan became their sole destination to safety.

During the ensuing months the organized freedom fighters and reinforcements from the north by the Russian Army reoccupied districts of Van and sporadic fighting never fully abated but eventually Van was lost. So as opposing forces took turns in short lived victories and defeats, the ordinary citizens were left with no choice except to depart.

Refugees fled the burning ruins of their lakeside paradise by every means possible. They left on horse and cart (araba) and horseback or on foot. Most headed for the high plains abutting Mount Ararat and the safe havens of Etchmiadzin and Yerevan. Bidding farewell to Van was a heartbreaking, tearful task. Van, Van, what have they done to you?

Chapter 33

Yeghishe and Satenig Escape Van

Satenig Gorgodian, a pretty, young adolescent girl of fifteen and a recent graduate of the Van school system was among the frenzied throng that abandoned their homes and their beloved city. The pert teenager left the besieged city with her father Ohaness, not yet sixty years old, but tired and feeble as a result of all his efforts to resist. Hripsimeh, his wife, was barely able to walk along the trail of escape. She was a fragile fifty years old, but her body belied her age. During the siege Hripsimeh had scrounged, scraped and skimped every scrap of food to help feed the fleeing masses of Vanetzsis that paused at the Gorgodian compound. She had not slept nor rested, but had persevered to be a "mayrig" (mother) for all the distressed who were forced to make the Gorgodian home a temporary shelter.

Satenig's brother Zaven and sister Kayane (with her children) completed the Gorgodian family exodus from Van. Somewhere, not far behind, followed young Yeghishe Catchouny. Throughout the arduous two week walk to the east, Yeghishe would find and walk alongside Zaven or Satenig. He became a constant roadside companion. The long and sometime broken serpentine line of Vanetzsis struggled slowly eastward. They shared whatever little food they had salvaged (mostly nuts and dried fruit). They lived off the land, searched out drinkable water and they slept beneath the cover of stars.

In this "highland wilderness" among the craggy hills near remote Kurdish settlements, the Armenian refugees faced the constant danger of attacks by pillaging bandit tribesmen. In one such village, Ishkir, Hripsimeh Gorgodian, weakened by illness, fatigue, starvation and thirst, surrendered her spirit to her Maker. She had fought the good fight, but she had nothing left to give. When the Gorgodians finally reached Etchmiadzin (some 30 or 40 miles short of Yerevan) the conditions of the family, as all the Vanities refugees, was appalling. The two week march from Van now humbled the exiled survivors to scavenge and then even beg for food, water and shelter. Throughout the march the exiles had clung together, supporting and comforting each other. They shed their tears and grieved the deaths of the weak, aged and very young. They were barely able to bury their dead in shallow graves or were forced to abandon the "fallen" at roadsides as they fled from the rain of Kurdish gunfire.

When Ohaness Gorgodian staggered into Etchmiadzin with his family, the ancient village was a crush of weary, bedraggled and in most cases, starving refugees. Etchmiadzin, of course, was the center and See of the Armenian Apostolic Church. The venerable Cathedral of Saint Gregory and home of the long line of Armenian Hairabeds or First Bishops.

Yeghishe Catchouny who had accompanied the Gorgodians fell severely ill shortly after arriving in Etchmiadzin. No doubt he had ingested some bad food or water. Yeghishe was forced to seek aid at a medical outpost and was only able to rejoin the family weeks later in Yerevan. The Gorgodians had no relatives or friends in Etchmiadzin so they were forced to sleep in the streets and scramble with the other exiles foraging for food and water.

Weeks earlier, during the siege of Van, Ohaness had opened the compound doors to many, many displaced Vanetzsis. The Gorgodian home was tucked away in the strictly Armenian sector of the Garden District. Its size and location made it "a safe house" for all the displaced Armenians who had evacuated their own homes in or about wards that adjoined the Turkish sector. The whole Gorgodian family had been overwhelmed in aiding frantic

Armenian families. During the last desperate days in Van, Ohaness not only shared his home, his food, and his goods, he chose to distribute all his money, his gold, silver and jewelry with his friends and neighbors.

Now, just a month later in the Holy City of The Illuminator, little was left to subsist. Ohaness was unwell, sorely weakened and distraught. He had just lost his life's mate Hripsimeh and the very lives of his children were at dire risk. His home and business were gone and his homeland, beautiful Van was in flames. But somehow, after a stay in Etchmiadzin of a few weeks, Ohaness had recovered enough and obtained (bought, bartered or borrowed) a horse and wagon.

According to Satenig, the family thought it prudent to bring the family cow with them as they fled from Van. The bovine would provide a mobile "nourishment station" for the needs of Kayane's young ones. It is probable that while in Etchmiadzin, the Gorgodians came to realize that they were unable to continue their journey to Yerevan on foot. In desperation did Ohaness trade their cow for transportation? In any case, together, worn and weary, with virtually no food or water, Ohaness, Zaven, Satenig, Kayane and her children left on their final frightful flight to Yerevan. Hripsime's remains were left buried, so, so sadly, miles behind, as were countless other victims of this continuing and mounting horror.

The city of Yerevan, at this point in time, was not in imminent danger of Turkish occupation. However, the masses of exiles seriously strained the capabilities of the city to care for all. After days of searching, Ohaness was able to find and rent "floor space" in a room of a terribly overcrowded apartment. Within weeks Ohaness, Kayane and two of her four children were destined to follow the fate of Hripsimeh. Death was a frequent visitor in 1915 Yerevan. Although I am again unsure of the details, the surviving two children of Kayane somehow escaped death.

During my first visit to Yerevan in 1996, I along with my wife Mary and my sister Mary were able to contact and spend an evening with the grandson of Kayane. He is a college professor and a prominent psychologist in a Yerevan Hospital. He is married and lives with his wife and son in the outskirts of the city. It was the day of the Blessing of the Holy Muron (oil) when we visited the home of Satenig's grand-nephew. My wife, my sister and I had spent a long day in Etchmiadzin but we looked forward to the evening gathering. We were warmly greeted and feted by the family with a grand Yerevantzi banquet dinner. As always "every Armenian guest is always honored as another Armenian's blood relative." There are no strangers in an Armenian household. During the darkest days of 1988, shortly after the earthquake and during the war of liberation in Karabagh, cousins Arax and Dick

Sarajian were able to get funds into Armenia to help this family survive. The Sarajians had continued to support their Yerevantsi cousins throughout the years which resulted in smiles of gratitude that glowed upon their faces when they hosted us. However, it seemed that in all of Yerevan, in 1996 the Armenians were still encumbered to don a dark shroud upon their shoulders. Perhaps it is only because their shoulders are strong enough to carry the burden. Their citizens never seem to lose hope or faith, or trust in God.

Shortly after the grievous death of four more family members, Zaven and Satenig found permanent housing at a distant cousin's home. Soon thereafter "big brother" found and enrolled Satenig into one of Yerevan's better public schools. Education was a priority. Even after the unspeakable hardships, Satenig needed to grow and prosper. She was now Zaven's responsibility.

Having settled his sister's affairs, Zaven received the exciting news that Russian reinforcements joined by Armenian guerilla fighters had reoccupied Van. After being assured of his sister's welfare, Zaven answered the rallying call for all able Vanetzsis to return to their home and to once again fight for Van.

During the fall of 1915 Yeghishe Catchouny was able to find a job as a teacher in Yerevan. Again as fate would have it another "mysterious coincidence" occurred. In the very same school

Yeghishe taught, young Satenig was a student. In 1916 two additional events of remarkable serendipity took place. One evening Satenig was called hurriedly to the door. She was excitedly told that her brother had returned and was there, at the doorstep. She expected to see Zaven, but it was not Zaven, it was Philip. Philip who had been trained and educated as a Turkish officer and of all things, was standing there dressed like a Kurd. Philip of course had been obligated to soldier as a Turkish Officer and had been posted near Kharpet when he was taken ill. While confined in a military hospital he was treated by a doctor who was Armenian. The doctor saw the young officer's dilemma and asked if he "wanted out" and then he arranged an escape plan. Dressed as a Kurdish woman Philip deserted his army post and made his way across a considerable stretch of Anatolia, first to Van and then to Yerevan. Satenig could hardly believe her eyes. Philip was alive, and here!

The happy and handsome youth was exhausted and the journey had left him grubby, heavily bearded and wholly unkempt. He was attired in a rough hewn tribal garb. He played the part well of an unsavory Kurdish clansman. Sadly, but heroically Philip's life was soon to end. In the spring of 1918, just after the Armenians declared themselves a free and independent Republic, Philip Gorgodian joined his bravest brothers in the Battle of Sardarabad. The Armenian forces under the command of Generals

Nazarabekian and Dro defeated an Ottoman military excursion which was determined to occupy Yerevan. The embryonic state of Armenia was saved from further Turkish intrusion. The Battle of Sardarabad had much to do with Armenia's independence. Philip Gorgodian gave all he had to insure Armenia's freedom. His name is now and forever emblazoned with the honored title of "Patriot of the Armenian Nation."

Chapter 34

Yeghishe Joins General Antranik

About the same time that Philip appeared in Yerevan, another young man was planning to desert the Turkish army. Sometime in early 1915 in Constantinople, Yeznik Catchouny was conscripted into the Turkish army. Attorneys were not exempt from military service, as were teachers, so Yeznik found himself on the "wrong side." Yeznik's army group was assigned to the (Russian) eastern front. At the first opportunity Yeznik surrendered to the Russian forces. He made it known that he was an Armenian who was forced to serve in the Turkish army. Yeznik was declared a prisoner of war but was permitted to contact Yeghishe in Yerevan. Yeghishe traveled to his brother's aid and was somehow able to arrange his release. The brothers Catchouny returned to Yerevan. Two stories have emerged concerning what Yeghishe and Yeznik did next. One story, inspiring, but probably untrue, was written in The Chronicles of the Prayer Beads. This tale reveals that the news announcing the date and details of Der Hoosig's death disturbed the two brothers so deeply that they immediately left Yerevan to join and fight with General Antranik.

The second version, from Satenig herself, recounts that neither Yeghishe nor Yeznik learned of their father's death until the war's end or possibly, not until early 1919. That version states that shortly after the Catchouny brothers' reunion the two boys were recruited by the Archbishop of Yerevan for an important task in Tiflis, Georgia. Tiflis, of course, had become the political and military headquarters for the exiled Armenian leaders. General Antranik himself was in Tiflis and he was in search of learned and astute patriots who could write, edit, publish and direct distribution of a newspaper mobilizing a new "striking force" for his volunteer army. Antranik met, interviewed and hired the brothers Catchouny to work toward that end.

The brothers fulfilled that role, but it did not quite end there. The quiet, scholarly, unassuming Yeghishe had much more to offer. After the launching of his newspaper and the successful appeal for fighting volunteers, Antranik sought the intellectual support and consul of Yeghishe Catchouny. The bright 27 years old lawyer-teacher from Arabgir, Bolis, Van and Yerevan was assigned the role of the General's traveling aide. Young Catchouny wrote and fought with Antranik, his own personal hero and ultimately became his confidant, historical-scribe and trusted representative. Antranik was already a mythical and fabled freedom fighter. His deeds of fearlessness were so daunting that he was even featured and regaled as a popular hero in America. Half a world away Antranik's feats appeared in an exciting pictorial column "Above the Crowd" in the N.Y. Journal American.

Antranik had been thrown into the "independence" fray as a youngster and consequently had only obtained a limited academic education. Now, years later, Antranik's unfailing instincts and dawning realization of his need for a helping "velvet glove" led the gruff, impatient and sometimes quarrelsome general to adopt Yeghishe as an invaluable advisor and devoted companion.

A collection of "Antranik insights" can be found in Yeghishe's book Travels with Antranik and the Lone Strike Division which was published in 1976 in New Jersey. Yeghishe's book was written in Armenian and later translated (but not completely) into English by Arthur Ayvazian. Among a deluge of other facts, the Ayvazian translation reveals that Antranik was greatly disappointed in the unfulfilled promises of support for his army he was assured from the leaders of the "National Council." According to the General, the lack of arms and manpower led to the fall of Garin (Erzurum) in early 1917 and later the surrender of Kars in April of 1918. Yeghishe's narrative delves into the genesis and the formation of the "Lone Strike Division" in Alexandrapol. The reading of the journal gave me a "feel" of peeking into Yeghishe's personal diary. It is an intimate and detailed account taking you to the very heart of the fight for independence.

I can only hope that sometime in the future, a skilled, erudite Armenian historian-archivist will find the means to probe the books and personal papers of Yeghishe Catchouny. He was the scribe, the reporter, the capturing eye of events that hunger to be read, analyzed, discussed and if possible, historically understood. The challenge is great, but so is the reward. A sacred page of Armenian history is awaiting exploration. All of Yeghishe's memoirs are a fascinating "time lapse" journal into Armenia's struggle for independence.[31]

While Yeghishe was occupied fighting with Antranik on the Eastern Front and in Karabagh, Satenig was experiencing her own adventures. The young teenager and her brother Zaven were forced to flee Yerevan when the Turks threatened the city. Together with their close knit band of Vanetzsis, the siblings Gorgodians charted a course to Tbilisi, Georgia. As the situation worsened and the Turkish armies advanced, Satenig and Zaven abandoned Georgia and trekked deeper into the ominous peaks and gorges of the Caucasus Mountains. During one especially remote mountain passage Satenig, Zaven and their group of young Armenian refugees were taken captive by a fearsome horde of brutish, hugely framed and heavily bearded Russian mountain men. Zaven and the rest of the Armenian men were "roughed up" and then bound together with coarse bristle ropes. The girls were separated, whisked away and confined in the custody of some "Amazonian" sized women.

The fate of all appeared bleak, when multi-lingual Krikor Vartanian, babbling in his broken Russian, finally made himself understood. These "wild and wooly men" of the Caucasus spoke an unusual "mountain dialect" of Russian, but few among their midst made sense of the Armenian's jabbering. They finally understood that these ragged captives were not Kurds or Turks, but were Christian Armenians fleeing from Islam. The once fierce and fearsome foragers of the Caucasus suddenly became warm and affectionate friends and compatriots. Their enemies were common – so these newly found comrades from the "High Caucasus" considered themselves to be brothers and sisters to the Armenians. The group feasted, slept and then passed in peace.

Satenig, Zaven and the rest eventually arrived at Rostov, Nakhichevan. Here they found an unexpected community of Armenians who welcomed and cared for them for the next ensuing months. Later in 1917 some of the men from their band of refugees decided to return south to Georgia or even (if possible) on to Armenia (Yerevan). When Zaven got news that Tiflis and Yerevan were safe, he too decided to return. He promised Satenig he would send for her when he got settled. Within a few months Satenig had heard from her brother and had the money and proper papers necessary to return to Yerevan. I have no information regarding her return trip so it must have been uneventful.

Once back in Yerevan, Satenig re-enrolled into the Hovnanian School. In short order she completed her remaining required courses and received her diploma. Yerevan exploded with excitement when in May of 1918 independence was declared and the first Republic of Armenia was born. Not a kingdom, but a Republic! Within weeks the spunky Satenig and her longtime friend and classmate Siroon Bedrosian applied for and were granted positions as secretaries, working for the newly formed Parliament of the Republic. What an honor. What an achievement.

Towards the final days of World War I, late in 1918, Antranik Ozanian submitted a plan to the Allied Command to assault Baku on the Caspian Sea. This carefully crafted strategic maneuver was immediately rejected. The French and English had already devised a political post-war scheme to partition and divide the Caspian oil fields. Antranik had been previously thwarted by politics in his own "backyard," and now was blockaded by the "Big Allied Powers." It seemed to him what the Turks could not do (defeat him), his own people did. The great General was disappointed and discouraged and eventually retired his mighty sword, surrendering it to the Catholicos in Etchmiadzin. He then discharged and dispersed his volunteer army. Zoravor Antranik would never fight again. After the war's end, the General was summoned to England. In Great Britain Antranik received a conquering hero's welcome. Wealthy Armenians and appreciative non-Armenians offered him substantial financial rewards. The famous financier and founder of the A.G.B.U. (Armenian General Benevolent Union), Nubar Pasha was especially generous. Antranik accompanied by his entourage of war-time companions including Yeghishe Catchouny, humbly refused any monetary gifts or presents directed at him personally. Instead he directed all prizes and monies designated for him to be utilized to help heal the crippled Armenian people and nation. Large sums of money had already accumulated, not only in England but world-wide. Antranik dispatched his trusted and faithful Yeghishe to open offices in Alexandropol, in the Republic of Armenia, and to formulate a system of fairly distributing funds to the destitute. Antranik was not only the brave warrior for the people; he was now also the compassionate benefactor of his wounded nation. What he had given in war, he now gave in peace – his all.

Alexandropol, located just north of Etchmiadzin, had always been a "hot bed" of revolutionary activity. In 1919 while Yeghishe was engrossed in his newly assigned responsibilities, the "hot-bed" was now acquiring a "red tinge." The Bolshevik Party and its manifesto were sweeping southward from Russia. Yeghishe, a seasoned veteran, was well prepared to recognize the early signs of insurrection. Russia was beginning to collect its chips for its union. Catchouny did not hesitate to close his office and relocated to Yerevan.

Chapter 35

Yeghishe and Satenig Reunite to Flee the Bolsheviks

After reestablishing his new post in the Capital, Yeghishe sought out his trusted friends and reunited with his brother Yeznik. Yeghishe identified the "Red" storm clouds on the horizon and began fortifying his position. It was not long before the Communists began to infiltrate, and revolt against the Republic.

In a depressed and almost hopeless state of mind, Yeghishe gathered his closest friends, including Satenig, and together with brothers Yeznik and Kourken once again fled from Yerevan. According to Satenig's own remembrances, "we walked for at least two weeks, over and around mountains, through the snow and ice. We were so very cold; we had little food, perhaps one boiled egg or a small piece of aged meat for each day." The cold, wet, exhausted group of ten re-refugees finally reached Meghri on the banks of the Arax River. Somehow this weary band acquired a rubber balloon raft and embarked on a southward drift towards Persia (Iran). Upon reaching the border they were faced with still more difficulty. Persian border guards demanded money from the men (not the women) as a requirement (baksheesh or bribe) to be allowed to cross into the country. The girls were permitted to enter Persia but they did not see the men for days. Finally the men casually strolled into the Arab border village seemingly unaware of any anxiety or concern they had caused to their female companions. The reunited group continued their journey by foot to Tabriz.

Their flight from Yerevan and the Bolsheviks was an astounding land, mountain, river and desert crossing of better than two hundred miles. Just consider the hardships of distance, and terrain exacerbated by the lack of food and water, of adequate clothing and dearth of shelter in the mountain freeze or desert fire-storm. Now you can begin to realize what these young men and women were made of.

After reaching Tabriz, Yeghishe was able to communicate with the officials of the Near East Relief Organization and received a "line of credit" to replenish his exhausted funds. Yeghishe was instructed to establish a hospital aid station and to provide help to destitute, homeless and ill Armenian exiles in the locale. In just a matter of months some of Yeghishe's traveling companions decided to return "home" to Yerevan. The news from Armenia had harkened the passing of immediate dangers from the "Reds." The Republic's red, blue and orange flag still flew.

After establishing the hospital in Tabriz, Yeghishe and Satenig decided to retrace their own footsteps to the north. Their travel arrangements are vague, but I'm inclined to believe Yeghishe utilized the last of his "London Near East Relief" funds for a part of their passage to return home. As it turned out Yeghishe stayed in Yerevan, but Satenig continued on to Tiflis to nurse her brother Zaven who had taken ill in Georgia. It was in Tiflis that Satenig received news of Philip's fate as her brother battled the Turks and gave his life helping to secure Eastern Armenia at Sardarabad. In two short years Philip Gorgodian went from a Turkish officer to a martyred Armenian patriot. In two short years Satenig had lost all her family except brother Zaven. This was War, spelled with a capital G (Genocide)!

Shortly after arriving in Yerevan Yeghishe received orders to return to England. The "Organization" as well as Antranik awaited news and a front-line accounting of Yeghishe's efforts on their behalf. In lieu of having contact with the "source" I can only surmise that Yeghishe, at this moment in time, made the most memorable decision of his life.

He was now thirty one years old, battle scarred and war weary. It seemed all his years had been punctuated by death rather than life. Yeghishe deftly detoured his passage to England through Tiflis and asked Satenig to accompany him. On video tape Satenig shyly recalls "that moment" as she "fluttered" with shock, surprise and disbelief. She also recalls that she happily accepted Yeghishe's proposal. This would prove to be more than "a trip" – it would go on to be a life's journey.

The couple traveled from Tiflis, through Batumn carefully avoiding the Bolsheviks and continued on to Constantinople, then to Bulgaria, Paris, and finally Manchester, England. In Manchester Yeghishe reported and concluded his duties for the Near East Relief Fund. He also published some of his early works. In October of 1921 Yeghishe and Satenig were married in Manchester, England. (October 1921 is the same month and year in which Avedis and Ardemis wed). The clergyman who performed the ceremony was Vartabed Balakian, and General Antranik Ozanian stood as the best man (Godfather), and his bride-to-be Nevart Kurkjian was the Godmother.

Chapter 36

Yeghishe and Satenig Come to America

Shortly thereafter the wedding of Antranik to Nevart took place in Paris. The best man was Nubar Pasha. I am pretty certain that my own mother, years ago, told me that the celebrant was the Archbishop Kibarian, Prelate of France. The very same former fierce freedom fighting Bishop of Shabin Karahisar.[32] The date of this wedding was May 15, 1922. Still another coincidence, as this is the birthday of my mom Ardemis, May 15, 1902.

After a short stay in France, the Ozanians returned to England and then departed with an entourage, including Yeghishe and Satenig, for America. The group left aboard the White Star's luxury liner "The Olympus" from Southampton on July 5, 1922 and arrived in New York City on July 11th. They traveled first class, no steerage for this assemblage. According to Arax Sarajian, the

Antranik entourage avoided the perfunctory stay over at Ellis Island. Traveling with a notable such as Antranik had its rewards. The General and his wife were afforded deluxe accommodations at the posh Hotel Seville in Manhattan. Crowds of admiring and enthusiastic thousands came to great and honor Armenia's most significant warrior. I remember my mother musing, "I wanted so badly to go to see him, to greet him to tell him who I was. He was not only our hero, he was a Shabin Karahisatsi. As a youth he stayed and slept in our home. He played with my mother Anna and my aunts. But, I was in my last weeks of pregnancy (with Dick) and was not able to go."

After reaching New York City the humble, quiet and unassuming Catchouny couple did not participate in the wild and festive welcome that the East Coast Armenians were showering upon Antranik. They were dealing with some excitement of their own.

The following episode is a wondrous tale about something good coming out of something bad. I am unsure of location but Yeghishe and Satenig were being questioned as to their qualifications to enter America. Whether it was in Southampton or New York, an immigration officer was about to deny the Catchounys entry into the United States. The problem was that both Yeghishe and Satenig were in possession of Persian Passports. At that period in time the lawful entry quota for Persian citizens to enter America had been reached. When it was discovered that both Yeghishe and Satenig had documentation proving they were born in Turkey, a new door suddenly opened. Turkey had an unfulfilled quota base and so the Catchouny's qualified. What a stroke of serendipity. Who would have ever thought that this evil nation that so endeavored to send Yeghishe and Satenig (along with all the other Armenians) to eternal paradise would be the instrument that opened the door for the couple to pass into an earthly paradise, America.

The purged couple, happy and safe in the cocoon of this free and promised land were greeted by Mr. Mardiros Malkonian, and immediately departed for Troy, N.Y. where they were reunited with Yeghishe's sister Marguerite. It was here in upstate New York where Yeghishe and Satenig began the rest of their lives.

More than nine thousand miles away, the political fibers of Yeghishe and Satenig's ancestral motherland were undergoing another kind of metamorphous. Unfortunately it was not a happy "rebirth." In 1915 Armenia had been crushed like a fragile dove by the cruel hand of the "caretakers" of its sacred soil. Then in 1918 it was resurrected. It soared aloft, injured and scarred for sure, but nevertheless alive and frisky as a fledgling eagle eager for freedom. Now in 1922 it was again transformed, trans-figured into a dour dove, a docile captive dove. A red veil covered its pen and silenced its sweet cooing song. But Armenia's destiny had yet to be written. Hayastan would rise again.

Chapter 37

In America

Yeghishe and Satenig arrived in New York City in July of 1922. They immediately went to Troy, N.Y. where they lived with Yeghishe's sister Marguerite.[33] After a short stay upstate they returned to New York City to find work. Yeghishe first took a job working as an embroiderer and then as a "spotter" in the clothes cleaning business. For a short period of time the couple moved to Asbury Park, New Jersey where Yeghishe tried his entrepreneurial hand in the hot hobby of the time, stamp collecting. A bit later they took up residence in Manhattan. In November of 1922 their lives were blessed with the birth of their first born, a daughter, Alice.

In January 1928 with Yeghishe and Satenig along with young Alice living in Brooklyn, Arax, their second daughter was born. The Catchouny

279

family shortly thereafter moved to Orange, New Jersey. It was here that Yeghishe and Satenig opened their dry cleaning store, Embassy Cleaners. The store was located on Cleveland Street in Orange, and the family lived nearby at 401 Main Street. The Catchouny apartment was not large. It had one bedroom, one bathroom, a living and dining room and a tiny kitchen. It was here on Main Street in Orange, N.J. where son Armen Antranig was born in August 1936.

In the early days Yeghishe and his friends played soccer. Yeghishe was instrumental in forming the Armenian General Athletic Union (A.G.A.U), in this country. Along with the H.M.M.M. or Homenitmen, these organizations served young Armenians as their "sporting clubs" in the United States. Yeghishe was also active in the Society of Arabkertsis. These social societies of citizens of one of the villages, town, or area of the "yergeer" (old country), were where diasporites could keep in touch with kinsmen and spend hours discussing politics or just reminiscing. Satenig was active in her General Society of Vasbouragan, (Vanetzsis). Both husband and wife enjoyed socializing with old and new immigrants to get the latest news. The Catchounys continued to maintain close relationships with Yeghishe's nieces, Nartouhi and Eliz and their families who lived in nearby Essex County, New Jersey.

Yeghishe worked in the store every day insisting on being attired in a white shirt and tie. Satenig helped with the sewing and she took charge of the store when Yeghishe routinely walked home for lunch. Yeghishe owned and worked the store until he was forced to retire after the amputation of his leg as a result of diabetes in 1958. He wrote the last of his memoirs <u>Travels with Antranik</u> shortly thereafter being encouraged and supported by his daughter Arax and son-in-law Dick.

Satenig was known for her creative touch. She grew African Violets, was a terrific cook (with Kufteh a specialty) and used her sewing and knitting skills to create dolls, puppets and other assorted items. In her late years these little treasures were sold at the "Golden Door" counters in Englewood, New Jersey. She was particularly well know for taking ordinary store dolls and dressing them up in hand sewn traditional Armenian costumes.

Satenig was a good Armenian cook. When madzoon (Yogurt) was not yet a mainstream part of the American diet, her family ate it homemade and plain. To help entice the younger children to eat this nutritious dish, Satenig added strawberry jelly (to sweeten it). Unknowingly Satenig created the first ever fruit flavored yogurt for her family. As is credited to many Armenian Medsmyrigs (Grandmothers), I am sure long before the advent of Dannon and all others.

Alice Catchouny married Vanig Hagopian in September 1944. Vanig, also of Vanetsis parentage, lived in Teaneck, New Jersey. While serving in the Army Air Corps during World War II, he was stationed in California. Vanig proposed to Alice and Alice, together with mom Satenig traveled cross country to California where Alice and Vanig were married. After the war Vanig and Alice settled first in Connecticut and ultimately in Bergenfield, New Jersey. Vanig was employed as a photoengraver and Alice worked for Scholastic Books. The Hagopians had two daughters Sona (born 1946) and Susan (born 1949). Sona attended Douglas College and married Daniel Stork (1964). Daniel earned his Ph.D. from New York University and became a professor at Smith College where Sona earned her degree. Presently the two live in Southern California. They have no children.

Susan graduated from Upsala College where she met Alan Baskin. The two married in August of 1972. Susan worked for the Social Security Administration. Alan was employed as an accountant. The couple moved to San Diego, California where they had two children, Joshua and Michael. Susan died of breast cancer in June 1988. Josh graduated from San Diego State (and also completed collegiate ROTC training). He entered the Army as a Lieutenant, but during a training jump with the airborne he suffered a serious injury and was medically discharged. Josh is presently living in

Israel, and was married in 2007. He has two daughters.

Michael was graduated from the United States Military Academy at West Point. After completing "Ranger" training he served in a combat group in Afghanistan. Michael has recently served our nation as a combat instructor and has achieved the rank of Captain. He also served two war-time tours of duty in Iraq.

Arax married Dick Sarajian in May 1951. They initially lived in Palisades Park, New Jersey. They brought their home in River Edge, New Jersey in 1954. Dick was a photoengraver for Pictorial Engraving. Later he became a principal in Pictorial, Powers, Conway and ultimately Gotham Graphics of Lyndhurst, New Jersey. As we have discussed, Dick passed away in July 2006. Dick and Arax have three children. Richard Haig (October 1951) graduated from Colgate University and Albany Law School of Union College. He is a partner in the law firm of Montalbano, Condon and Frank, P.C. Richard married Nora Daghlian, a civil engineer, in 1987. The couple have four sons: Ara (1988), Raffi (1991), Garo (1992), and Haig (1996).

Kenneth Armen (May 1953) was graduated from Franklin and Marshall College and the American University (M.P.A.). He has been a teacher, a coach, worked in administration and sales at Gotham Graphics, and had a career in the IT Industry. He is presently engaged as a History

Teacher at Pascack Valley High School in New Jersey. Ken married Patricia (Trish) Driemeyer (an H.R. Professional) in 1991. They have two children, Ani (1993), and Stephen (1994).

Carol Susan (August 1957) was graduated from Georgetown University. Carol was development officer for a college and dental school, and presently works in a bank's H.R. department. Carol married James (Jim) Kennelly (1984). Jim has a recording studio "Lotas Productions." They have two sons Michael James (1989) and Daniel (1992).

Armen Antranig Catchouny attended Upsala College and worked for Budweiser, the U.S. Postal Service and ultimately as a supermarket inventory officer. Armen married June Raymond (a nurse) in 1959. Armen passed away in May 1999. Armen and June have three children, Patricia Elisa (April 1960), attended Upsala College and is an insurance professional in Syracuse, New York. She is well known in the community for her producing, directing and acting skills in regional theater. Thomas Armen (May 1962) passed away in September 1998. Amy Laurig (July 1966) attended Upsala College and is a paralegal at a New Jersey law firm.

Author's Note:

When I began to expand my narrative of the Sarajian and Sergenian families it was my intention to use the "Khnamies" to provide another perspective of the Survivors of the Genocide. My entry into the world of Yeghishe and Satenig has proved to be an unexpected roller coaster ride for me. I encountered some expected barriers, but even more so, I kept on confronting "forks in the road." To paraphrase Yogi Berra's edict, "I took them-all of them." I do hope you will excuse my "expansiveness" in dealing with their lives. I began writing the Catchouny segment with a scarcity of facts. Somehow after searching, uncovering, extruding, compiling, correlating and finally putting it all down on paper I ended up with an unedited script of ponderous proportions. I will "lean" on my daughter to help "clean" out the work. The truth is that often I discovered sources of information I did not know even existed. I found myself entangled in a web of captivating flights, escapes, and adventures of a couple I had known for years, but never really knew. Again, I am sure I have used this phrase before; these were ordinary people, who led extraordinary lives. How uncommon was it that in an era of repeated coincidences their struggles in Turkey were solely unique. When families were being divided, couples forever separated, these two found unity. Their lives so paralleled each other's that their destiny was almost inevitable or predictable. These two friends shared so many of their exile experiences that they were "joined" in the drama of life before they were "joined" on the altar of wedlock. Yeghishe and Satenig were heroes of their time. All our Survivors were heroes for sure but history, (or call it fate) seems to thrust a select few to act as "front-line" witnesses. Those two walked in and amongst the footsteps of Aharonian, Dro, Sebouh, Murad, Antranik, and the Republic's first Parliament. They were also "selected" to be present and to observe the rise and fall of the first Republic. However they were not merely observers of Armenian History, they were active participants.

You, their offspring and heirs, can look back and now appreciate the depth of the battles, the strength and honor of their unbowed heads. I think the Catholicos of Cilicia, Aram the First, put it at his eloquent best when he spoke of the Survivors of the Genocide. He said "They are not only a part of our history; they are a part of our daily lives." And so they are - and so they are.

Chapter 38

The Kachians

A.   Mgrditch Kachian

Mary Kachian, when she began dating Haig Sarajian in 1960, was a vivacious Armenian-American girl living in New York City. Mary had grown up a first generation "Hye" with her roots deeply ingrained in the culture of her Armenian heritage. Through her church and various ethnic activities, Mary was acquainted with Dick and Mary Sarajian before she ever met Haig. Mary was the oldest child of Mgrditch and Rahan Kachian.

Mary lived with her parents, together with her sister Berjouhi, and her brother Mardig. The patriarch and matriarch of the family, Garabed and his wife Kohar (Mgrditch's parents) completed the family unit.

In the 1950's the family lived in a stately and sturdy brick home on the cliffs overlooking the Harlem River in the Bronx. The house was but a stone's throw away from the George Washington Bridge. Both Mary's parents and grandparents had suffered as victims and survivors of 1915 and the dark desolate days that followed the Genocide. Their personal odyssey took them on different routes from the hilltop villages about Palu, through the desert cities of Syria and Lebanon and finally to the alabaster skyscrapers of New York City.

It was 1915 and Mgrditch, a boy of thirteen and Rahan, a child of just four, were both forced to flee from their homes and eventually from their ancestral birthplaces of Palu Havav and Palu Sigham. They escaped the sword and shot of the Turk but not without suffering much pain and anguish. The chaos and mayhem about them carved an indelible, inextinguishable nightmare into their psyche and souls. Even years later, when safe in each other's loving care, and protected within the sanctuary of America, their old wounds remained open sores festered by their tears, which never, ever ceased. Their story is unique in its detail and substance, but it is strikingly familiar in its essence. A heartache which is a gripping adjunct to the Sarajian-Sergenian-Catchouny and Gorgodian saga. Sadly it is an unsatisfied, yet to be fulfilled chapter in the chronicled history of the genocide. Closure, finally salved with disclosure, followed by repentance and reparation is an epilogue all Armenians await.

In 1915 Garabed Kachian (Mgrditch's father) was in America trying to find the means to rescue his family from Ottoman Turkey. The conditions in his home village of Havav made his desperate fight a last chance. Garabed's wife Kohar and their young son Mgrditch were anxiously awaiting news from Garabed in America while the situation in Turkey was worsening. Kohar was suffering terribly. She lamented the death of two of her four children and her eldest, Mary sought the refuge of a Kurdish marriage to save her life. Recent rumors in Havav told of atrocities which were being committed upon the Armenians by the military in nearby villages. The few remaining friendly Kurds were no longer viewing the Armenians as neighbors and friends. Instead, the Turks were encouraging the Kurds to claim Armenian land and property as their own.

In the spring of 1915, amongst all the villages in the Palu district, the Ottoman government posted their official edict ordering the immediate exile of all Armenians. In effect and practice, this single simple directive to "evacuate and relocate" sealed the mandate to scatter, dispose and annihilate the remains of the Christian Armenian race in Turkey. The manner of the banishment was unwritten but well understood. The Armenians were legally injuncted to be marched into oblivion.

As soon as the "evacuation" order came down, Kohar and young Mgrditch became separated in the mass turmoil and confusion. While searching for Mgrditch, Kohar became trapped by a Turkish band of military brigands and was found hiding behind some bedding and comforters in a neighbor's home. She was captured with other women and children who were "apprehended" and then all were routed from Havav and driven like cattle to a hilltop. There they were ordered to undress completely, herded into an open field, and all were shot. Those who survived the barrage of lead were brutality bayoneted.

Kohar was shot through the chest and was abandoned for dead. In the gruesome, mangle and tangle of desecrated flesh, she somehow survived. After dark, Kohar crawled out of this nightmare. She found a scrap of clothing to cover herself and made her way to the home of a Kurd who had taken an Armenian for his wife. The man had also been a friend to Kohar's husband Garabed.

The Kurd, in spite of being fearful of Turkish reprisals against any who aided Armenians, relented and permitted Kohar to seek the shelter of his barn. It is impossible to describe the agony and hardships Kohar endured while hiding in this barn. She tended to her gunshot wound herself, without medicines, bandages or water. Slowly, she healed and when she felt strong enough she left the relative safety of her Kurdish neighbor and went her own way. Soon, she was found by another Kurd and subjugated to accept his proposal to be his Moslem wife (and slave). This was another case of "be wed or be dead." Kohar needed to survive, her son Mgrditch was out there somewhere.

We cannot be sure of how much time passed in service to this Kurd, but Kohar regained both her strength and resolve and again escaped. She now began her determined drive to find her son.

Meanwhile, back in a village near Havav, Mgrditch had himself defied death on more than one occasion. During the gathering stage of the evacuation order Mgrditch was adopted into an elderly Kurd's home. The Turkish command ordering the exile of Armenians was quite explicit on their orders, and any aid offered to an Armenian was punishable by death. However to some Kurds occasional risks were necessary if for no other reason, to stay alive. The aged Kurd who claimed Mgrditch was too feeble to work his land and farm by himself. In effect he and his wife were doomed to a slow death without help. He saw young Mgrditch as his prayer to Allah answered. To his misfortune, within a few days his work horse was discovered, dragged away and held captive along with six other bedraggled Armenian boys.

The gendarmes were quick to dispense Islamic justice, and either by blade or bullet the first six youths were "dispatched." But, before the gunman could pull the trigger on Mgrditch, the old crippled Kurd hobbled into their midst. He made a frantic scene wailing and weeping. Doubtlessly he took this daring gamble because his crime of harboring Mgrditch carried a death sentence. The old man bemoaned his own miserable existence and emphasized his dilemma and supplication by kissing the boot of the "headman". With cries of hopelessness, the old Kurd beseeched the leader that he and his wife could not survive without the help of this "Gavoor" boy. The gendarmes were sympathetic to the old-timer and relented. With a typical Turkish sneer the leader gifted life to both the terrified Armenian lad and to the craggy old Kurdish farmer.

Mgrditch worked hard for his master. Of course, he was unaware but apprehensive as to the fate of his mother or other family members. His world had been turned upside down. Many months passed and while in the fields Mgrditch made contact with other village youths who were in similar circumstances. In time some Armenians attempted to flee from the captive safety of their Kurdish farmers. The risk of capture was great, and the penalty usually meant death. But the lure of reuniting with loved ones remained overpowering. Amongst the Armenian "adoptees" a crude network was formed, and every opportunity for a successful escape was examined.

One fall day while working the fields together with his Kurdish master, Mgrditch saw a body lying on the banks of a nearby creek. The man and boy approached the prone figure and in horror Mgrditch recognized the ragged, unconscious female figure to be his aunt Zahrou, the wife of his father's younger brother.

His father's brother, Khougas, had joined his brother Garabed in America. Upon hearing of the Armenian Massacres, Khougas, not heeding the advice of Garabed, would journey back to Turkey. While searching for his family in his home village of Havav, Khougas was spotted, shot and killed. It's not known whether he ever discovered the fate of his wife or his two martyred sons.

As for his wife Zahrou, she had been saved by another "benevolent" Kurdish family. When she became too weak to work because of constant beatings, malnutrition and illness, she was turned out, ejected, cast away as you would an unwanted sick cat or dying dog. Lying almost dead at creek-side, Zahrou was a sorry sight. Mgrditch begged his Kurdish lord to permit him to nurse her back to health. This would be a great benefit for the farmer, for now he would have two workers and could lead an easier life. Mgrditch promised he would share his meager portions of food so in effect the Kurd would not bare any extra expense. The Kurd agreed. Zahrou was saved and with much loving help from Mgrditch in time she recovered.

The months and seasons passed, and one spring day plans were formulated among the Armenian contingent to attempt an escape. Their mindset was to reach Kharpet and Mezre where they had heard that many Armenian refugees had found shelter. They would then seek aid, and begin the search for family members. Mgrditch and Zahrou made their getaway and banded together with their group seeking freedom.

On the backroads to their destination, perhaps many miles away, the resolute brothers and sisters were sighted by an army patrol. They scattered, were pursued and fired upon, and at least one of their numbers was hit and killed. Good fortune again smiled on Mgrditch as he and Zahrou avoided any further confrontations and made it safely to Kharpet.

Months earlier Kohar had made her escape from her Kurdish "husband". She had spent months searching through the villages and villyets of Palu looking for Mgrditch. She eventually arrived in Kharpet.

Even here, in the twin cities of Kharpet and Mezre, Kohar could not find Mgrditch. She was exhausted from her search and decided to stay here and await news. She found work in the local farms and lived the life of a Kurdish field woman. We are not sure how mother Kohar and son Mgrditch were finally reunited. We do know that once reunited, they lived together, apart from Zahrou "Hachook" (brother-in-law's wife). All three remained in Kharpet until the end of World War I in 1918.

The defeat and subsequent occupation of Turkey opened the channels to active communication between the Armenians in the Diaspora and their decimated families in Anatolia. Garabed Kachian received the miraculous news that his wife and son were alive and safe in Kharpet. Kohar was still a field worker and Mgrditch had found work as a shoemaker's assistant. He was now sixteen years old. Garabed's efforts to provide immigration papers for both his wife and son were not successful. It was not until 1920-1921 when under the new repressive regime of Ataturk, Mustafa Kemal, that Turkey permitted (actually encouraged if not forced) the exodus of the battered and scattered remnants of the ravaged Armenian population.

Garabed made plans to bring his family to America. He was also able to arrange a mail order agreement between a friend Baron Vartian and his slain brother's wife, Zahrou. The two would wed if she agreed to accept Vartian's offer to pay her passage to the United States.

Mail-order brides were the primary means available to single or widowed Armenian men to restart a "Hye" (Armenian) family. About the same time Kohar, together with 18 year Mgrditch left Turkey for nearby Aleppo, Syria. Then, they continued on to Beirut, Lebanon. In Beirut, Kohar received both the money and documentation necessary to immigrate to America and reunite with her husband Garabed. The year was 1921 and the couple had been apart for almost a decade.

Mgrditch, now 19 years old was once again forced to live apart from his parents. He remained behind in Beirut because of age restrictions in the United States immigration code. He was now working as a house builder, a craft he happily enjoyed as an avocation for the rest of his life.

Years passed, and at last in 1926 Mgrditch made the crossing to America. He had received papers identifying him as Tatoul Kachian, his deceased younger brother. Mgrditch now a handsome man of 24 had not seen his father for some 12 years. Garabed and Kohar had not failed him. With hope, effort and pride the Kachian family came together again. With boundless courage they were able to leave their terrors and tears ten thousand miles behind them. But the insidious shadow of the Turk must have haunted them for the rest of their days.

Chapter 39

Rahan Delerian

Early in the spring of 1915, in the small village of Sigham in central Turkey, Rahan Delerian had just celebrated her fourth birthday. Rahan, named for Basil, the first plant that had grown on Jesus Christ's grave (as she told the story), lived with her father Mardiros, a tall handsome man who was now in his early forties. Mardiros was a respected educator, a professor at the Euphrates College of Kharpet. Rahan's mother, Altoon Gulazian Delerian, had died during the birth of Rahan's brother Kourken in 1913, when Rahan was just 2 years old. Shortly thereafter Mardiros had remarried and his wife quickly had a daughter.

Rahan's sister, Marinos, was 14 years her senior. Shortly before the outbreak of World War I, Marinos had married Hovanness Goomishian. Since

Mardiros was gone for long periods of time to work at the college, Hovanness remained at home to help run the farm. The house and land owned by the Delerians was substantial. The family farmed grain and vegetables and had livestock and fruit orchards. Since Sigham was almost a completely Armenian village, much of the fieldwork was provided by Kurds or Turks who lived just beyond the town boundaries. The villagers all spoke Armenian, had their own school and church.

Sigham was located just over the mountain from the district governing township of Palu, and a few miles beyond was the city of Kharpet with its sizable Armenian population. The relationship between the Armenians and the Kurds was somewhat interdependent since both minorities shared the soil as a subject people to the Ottoman Turks. As neighbors in a hostile environment, the Moslem Kurds and Christian Armenians, for most part, were cordial. However, the Kurds were often known to harbor a jealous eye towards the enterprising Armenians.

Soon after Marinos' wedding to Hovanness, Mardiros sensed the impending danger in Turkey. Mardiros offered to send Hovanness to America to prepare the way for the entire family to emigrate out of the Ottoman Empire. Hovanness became the family's lifeline to freedom.

In the early spring of 1915 there arose a significant tension between the Moslem population and the Armenians. Once the order confirming the compulsory exile of all Armenians was posted, Sigham was transformed into a lawless and brutalized community. Each hour brought forth new outbursts of violence. Rahan recalls that is was as if the Kurds "had lost their minds." Along with the few Turks in town, the Kurds pillaged, looted, ravaged and raped. Homes were torn apart in search of hidden gold and jewelry. Turks and Kurds torched churches filled to the rafters with cringing Armenian Christians to the ground.

The Armenian districts became burning, barbarous war zones with death as an expedient substitute for the order to relocate. In the midst of all this bedlam, Mardiros made hasty preparations for his family to flee. Before he could even gather his family, he saw the approach of rampaging gendarmes. Mardiros sensed their only purpose. He bolted out the rear door and made a run for the shelter of the nearby forest. But he was spotted and pursued by a shouting band of Turkish soldiers and Kurdish "irregulars."

Within minutes, Rahan heard shots in the distance. She remained hidden with her big sister Marinos. After a short time, Marinos and Rahan left their home and followed the trail beyond the fields and into the forest. They searched for their father. Horrifically, they found his beheaded body and head. In profound grief, and shock, the two sisters clawed the rocky soil with bare and bloodied fingers. In loving tears, and bereft of formal ceremony or clergy, the girls conducted their makeshift burial service for their father. In heartbreaking anguish they placed Mardiros' head in its grave site.

Marinos and Rahan left the nightmare of the woods and carefully made their way back to the ravaged village. There they found their little brother Kourken and fled into the mountains of Palu. In time, the sisters reached the home of an Agha and Hannum (Lord and Lady), in the town of Palu. This was an influential man who had married an Armenian girl. Marinos knew that he was also a friend of her father's.

The girls were taken in, and given sanctuary with a large number (about nineteen) of other Armenian children. The group lived and worked in the home and fields of the Agha, but food was scarce and living difficult. Rahan recounted how they were given a small piece of bread to last the entire day. They fed their gnawing hunger with grass from the fields. They were given little water and as a result were made to drink the dirty water that ran down the drainpipes of the house. Sickness and death were prevalent.

Marinos worked in the home and Rahan was assigned the role of shepherdess. Rahan cannot recall all that took place during these last years of World War I. Tearfully she does remember that her baby brother died early in the stay at the Agha's home. Rahan attributed his death to starvation.

When the war came to a close in 1918, relief stations and orphanages appeared throughout Turkey. The Armenians' plight was well documented by news reports. Some attempts to give aid to the "Starving Armenians" were headlined. The sponsors to administer aid to the Armenians included religious organizations, such as the Protestant and Catholic groups. These groups provided aid and solace almost as a substitute for the decimated Apostolic Church of the Armenians. Of course, the Red Cross contributed as did national and political aid societies such as Near East Relief.

In late 1918 and early 1919 a number of orphanages opened in the twin cities of Kharpet and Mezre. Hearing of this, and now seeking to rekindle their Armenian heritage and escape the Agha, Marinos took Rahan, now seven years old, to a facility in Mezre. The two sisters were among the first to enter the all girl orphanage funded by the Apostolic Church. The Armenian Patriarchy in Constantinople was faced with the overwhelming task of reuniting its charges with their families.

Safe shelters like those in Kharpet and Mezre beckoned runaways to start life anew as Armenian Christians. In 1919 life in the orphanage of Mezre was not easy. Food and clothing were scarce and the youngsters battled just to survive. Rahan recalls that for many months her daily ration of food was a wineglass of cooked chickpeas. Whatever else entered her stomach was scrounged from the ground behind the walls of the orphanage.

Marinos, weak from hunger and sick with asthma decided to return to the home of the Agha in Palu. Rahan supposes that Marinos' age, now twenty-two, may have caused the orphanage to encourage her to leave. In Palu, under the care of the Agha's second wife, she regained her strength. Marinos was also able to resume a correspondence with her husband in New York City.

Back in Mezre the conditions gradually improved in the orphanage. In 1920 - 1921 the President of the new Turkish Republic, Mustafa Kemal urged all Armenians to leave Turkey. As Turkey extricated itself from the occupation of Allied Forces in 1920, a new series of cruelties and killings erupted against Christians across Anatolia. With fear of blame and renewed reprisal for the lost war, the Armenians in Turkey expedited their exodus from their ancient homeland.

In Mezre immediate plans were made to close the orphanage. Rahan was whisked away in a horse and wagon with a small contingent of young girls and a few teachers. They joined a host of other Armenians and crossed the border to Aleppo, Syria.

After a short stopover in Aleppo, the group continued on to the Catholicate of Antilias located outside of Beirut in Lebanon. Here the girls were interviewed and vital information was noted. Then the orphans were categorized and separated according to age and other factors. Efforts were made to contact relatives and to reunite families.

Rahan, now about ten years old, was sent to a Mediterranean seaside orphanage in the village of Saida just outside Beirut. Life improved dramatically in Saida. The Near East Relief Organization provided an abundance of food and clothing. The girls were well cared for, and they all attended school according to age and ability. Rahan enjoyed being near the sea and her love of the ocean would last her whole life.

During her stay in Lebanon, Rahan was transferred twice more to different facilities. First she was sent to an orphanage in the village of Jounieh and then to a second orphanage in Saida, this one on a "hilltop". Rahan recalled that each "home" was comfortable and that the staff and teachers of the children were caring and protective. During the next few years Rahan grew, made friends and continued to write notes to Marinos in Turkey.

In Palu, besides keeping in touch with Rahan, Marinos anxiously awaited news from her husband Hovanness. Hovanness was now living in New York City after his discharge from the United States Army. He made initial contact with Marinos through the Armenian "search" network, which buzzed with information after the end of the war. Using his newly acquired influence as an U.S. citizen, Hovanness explored the possibility to "extricate" his wife from the interior of Turkey. Somehow he managed to convince the Embassy that she was too ill to travel alone, and a representative was sent to Palu to escort her out of Turkey.

Marinos, as the wife of an American citizen was entitled to the privileges and protection of a citizen. Preparations were made for her journey. Around this time an American doctor had seen Rahan at the orphanage in Beirut and inquired about the possibility of an adoption. Marinos (still responsible for Rahan) refused to give permission, rationalizing that she and Hovanness, together in America, would bring Rahan safely to their sides.

Marinos made arrangements to remove Rahan from the orphanage and return her to Aleppo where she had contacted an aunt (her father's sister, another survivor from Sigham). Rahan agreed to move and made the journey back to Aleppo. She was greeted by Aunt Goulpik and her family. She lived with them for one year, attending the Haigazian Armenian School.

Marinos reunited with her husband in America after a separation of some seven or eight years. Hovanness and Marinos sent funds to Aunt Goulpik so that Rahan could attend the school and further her education. Marinos could not convince the embassy to permit Rahan's immigration. Rahan was now about fourteen or fifteen years old. Marinos directed Rahan to leave Aleppo and travel back to Beirut and find her Aunt Mariam. This aunt was the sister of Altoon, their mother who had died in 1913. Mariam had escaped the horrors of Sigham and resettled in Beirut. Rahan made the journey alone and found another family in Beirut.

Aunt Marian lived with her two daughters and she too awaited news from her husband who had escaped to America. Rahan found work in bustling Beirut making leather satchels. Her boss was quite old but took an immediate liking to this little orphaned girl. He was kind and caring of her needs. Finally, in 1928 the good news came from America. Hovanness' uncle was returning to America from Greece, and would pass through Marseilles. At the same time Hovanness and Marinos had somehow arranged to adopt Rahan as their daughter, making her a United States citizen. Marinos had sent papers to the embassy in Marseilles, France. In Beirut, Mariam put Rahan on a ship bound for Marseilles.

Rahan lived in France for three months with the Der Manuelian family until Hovanness' uncle and aunt arrived from Greece. The uncle took Rahan to the embassy and made arrangements for her to leave France accompanied by him and his wife. They traveled overland to the coast and boarded the ocean liner "Olympic" bound from Cherbourg to New York, traveling in second class.

Chapter 40

Rahan in America

In August 1928 Rahan Delerian left Cherbourg, France for America. During a particularly rocky crossing across the Atlantic, Rahan suffered severe seasickness. She was taken to the ship's hospital which was adjacent to the first class cabins. She recovered quickly and on August 30, 1928 she arrived at Ellis Island in New York Harbor. Rahan's stay was a short one at Ellis Island, just twenty-four hours, because her papers identified her as a United States citizen.

With tears of joy and happiness, Rahan was at last reunited with her sister Marinos. She had been separated from Marinos for seven years and had not seen Hovanness for almost fifteen years. Rahan was just shy of her eighteenth birthday. Marinos, her sister, was thirty years old. Marinos' life in America would be short, for she died at the age of forty-two leaving behind Hovanness and a young son Khachig.

Rahan took residence with Marinos and Hovanness in their tenement apartment on East 47th Street. Marinos and Hovanness were proprietors of a small grocery store (this is long before the age of supermarkets). Not having enough work for three at the store Rahan with her limited English (learned in the orphanages) was quick to find work in the manufacturing district of the city. Her first job was making and assembling lampshades and later she worked at a factory making bed sheets. Like most immigrants Rahan's employment opportunities improved as her network of friends expanded. Eventually she found work in a dress factory with her fellow "Palutsi" Mary Sarkisian (later Masoian).

Besides introducing Rahan into the world of dressmaking, Mary had another introduction in mind. The year was about 1929 or early 1930 and Mary had an unmarried cousin who also was a Palutsi and a grocery storeowner as well. The man's name was Mgrditch Kachian. Rahan remembers him as ruggedly handsome with a shock of black hair and a pair of glowing eyes that seemed a shade darker than his hair. His character was as solid as his build. He lived with and supported his parents. Mary Sarkisian envisioned the blossoming beauty Rahan with this princely catch Mgrditch.

At a Christening party for George Maksian, later a well-known journalist with the New York News, Mgrditch finally met Rahan. It would be a new beginning for them. This first meeting and subsequent courtship took place between Rahan and Mgrditch in 1930. In June of 1931 the two were wed at St. Illuminators' Armenian Cathedral on 27th Street in Manhattan. The newlyweds honeymooned at The Shady Hill House in Hunter, New York. The hotel was located in the popular Catskill Mountain region of New York State.

The owners of this mountain resort, Mr. and Mrs. Tutunjian, were survivors of the Armenian Genocide as well. Mrs. Haigouhi Sergenian Tutunjian, the proprietress of the lodge, was a heroine from the battle on the pert at Shabin Karahisar, and a cousin to Ardemis Sergenian Sarajian. Who would know that almost 30 years later the children of Rahan and Ardemis would marry?

In 1931, in spite of the dawning of the Great Depression, Mgrditch and Rahan delved into their new life together with joy, energy and enthusiasm. Mgrditch and Rahan owned a series of grocery stores in both Manhattan and the Bronx. Each move was a notch in their climb into financial independence. Mary was born in 1932, Berjouhi two year later in 1934. Mardig (Mardiros, named for Rahan's father) was their last born in 1937.

Mgrditch's parents, Kohar and Garabed, handled much of the work on the home front, while the young couple put in long hours at the store. The children all went to college with both Berjouhi and Mardig being graduated with honors. The enterprising Mgrditch was among the very first of the immigrants to own his own car. The family even delved into the stock market and real estate; investments unusual for the generally conservative and careful Armenian businessmen of the late 30's and 40's.

In the late 40's the Kachians bought a stately brick home overlooking the Harlem River in the Bronx. The house abutted a large plot of land. Garabed soon put it to good use by planting and tending an extensive and flourishing vegetable garden.

The entire family was deeply involved with the Armenian Church and Armenian cultural affairs. In 1949 Kohar, who was a bit older than her husband, passed away. She was in her early 70's. Garabed died in 1958, still a handsome and vibrant man with a full head of snow-white hair, he was in his late 70's. Both senior Kachians were placed to rest in a grave at Cedar Grove Cemetery in Flushing, New York.

In late 1960, Mgrditch, who had retired just a bit earlier, decided he needed to get back into business. He bought a forty-room hotel, The White Swan, in Asbury Park, New Jersey, less than two blocks from the ocean. Sadly Mgrditch's dream of running this hotel at the seashore was short-lived. In March of 1964 Mgrditch Kachian died at home, as a result of a massive heart attack. His family gathered around him. His funeral and burial were conducted on Good Friday, March 24th 1964. He was put to rest in the family plot at Cedar Grove. He was only 62.

Mgrditch's legacy began as a boy with the spirit and courage he exhibited as a child. He faced and overcame a constant barrage of dangers, which at times left him almost hopeless, and in despair. He starred death in the face and was miraculously one of those who would be saved. Although Mgrditch would be scarred for the rest of his years by the tumultuous terrors no human should ever encounter, he persevered.

Perhaps Mgrditch's success in America was due to the conditioning he endured as a youth. Maybe the terrible frights he was exposed to a boy left him "immune" for whatever else life had to offer. Apparently he was fearless in facing the challenges of his immigrant life. He easily adapted to America. He quickly acquired business savvy and skills. As many Armenians, he had a knack for learning a strange new language. He became a stalwart leader in his church and community. He had the innate abilities to be a trendsetter rather than a follower. He did it all with quiet grace and dignity. He was as much at ease when facing a cranky customer in his store, as he was in solving a plumbing or electrical crisis in his home. Above all else, Mgrditch was a tireless provider and a deeply loving son, husband and father.

I was fortunate to know him as his son-in-law, his "pesah." But I was treated more like a son than an in-law. I can recall that evening well over forty years ago when we sat, face to face on a sofa in his home. It was the night we both knew I would ask for his blessings and permission to wed his daughter Mary. I'm not sure who perspired more profusely as I stammered my intentions to this gentle man. I do remember that he quickly gave his approval and then wrapped his arms about me in an embrace of happiness. We experienced joy for the marriage to be, but also because we both were so relieved that we had survived that intense and intimate moment.

What also comes to mind, sadly, is that just two or three years later the family would bid farewell to this wonderful man. On the day of Mgrditch's "Hoki Josh" (memorial dinner) a large crowd was gathered in the Kachian home in the Bronx. I found myself seated between two clerics, one our pastor, Hayr Krikor, and next to him another young Vartabed (celibate priest). The second priest, 23 years old, was a friend of Hayr Krikor and had assisted in the funeral service. He had "Havavtsi" roots as well. He was studying at Princeton University for his doctorate in Theology.

We would get to know him much better in time, as he went on to become an Archbishop and for twenty years our Prelate, His Eminence Mesrop Ashjian. Through those years he would be loved and respected by all that knew him. Sadly, with so much more to contribute to his people, the Archbishop died in December of 2003. He was just 62 years old; the exact age of Mgrditch Kachian whose final mass was celebrated that day in 1964.

As for our pastor from St. Illuminator's Hayr Krikor who also sat alongside me during the memorial dinner, he was destined to leave the priesthood. His calling was in a different direction as Krikor Pidedjian and Berjouhi Kachian (my sister-in-law) were wed in October of 1964. Both Krikor and Berjouhi are greatly gifted and talented. Together and individually they have contributed much in the field of education and especially in music. For more than forty years they have provided as educators, performers, and innovators in the Armenian-American cultural arena. Krikor has discovered and preserved long forgotten Armenian musical pieces. He has composed and conducted Armenian musical pieces in this country (including at the New York World's Fair) and in Armenia. Berjouhi's soprano voice has graced many of our churches and Cathedrals. She performed in this country and Armenia, and has sung throughout the chapels and standing ruins of Anatolia. She has sung where no Armenian voice has been heard in more that eighty years. Together they have been a cultural presence in the American-Armenian musical scene.

Chapter 42

Rahan without Mgrditch

Widowed at the age of fifty-three, Rahan never let adversity interfere with her energy. Alone she continued Mgrditch's dream as owner and proprietor of the White Swan Hotel in Asbury Park, New Jersey. When conditions deteriorated in Asbury Park during the 1970's, Rahan sold the White Swan. She had continued to live at the Sedgwick Avenue home she shared with Mgrditch. Berjouhi, Krikor and their two young sons, Datev and Antovk now lived there as well. As Berjouhi worked full-time as a teacher, Rahan undertook the responsibility her mother-in-law Kohar had assumed a generation earlier and watched the children while their mother was at work. Her early influence with the boys was supremely beneficial. Today Datev is a pediatrician, married to Jeanne Minassian, and the father of

Alexandra, Adam and Stephan. Antovk became an attorney, married Ani Hadjian, and in May, 2006, became a father to Kyle Vahan. Both Pidedjian boys share a great love for their Medz-Mayrig (grandmother).

During these years, Rahan's other children prospered as well. Her first daughter, Mary, married me, Haig Sarajian, and we blessed her with two more grandchildren, Nadine and Michael. Nadine, Rahan's only granddaughter, always looked up to her grandmother as the supreme role model. Nadine went on to become an attorney and marry Gregor Koobatian a physician. Nadine and Greg have three wonderful children, John, Elizabeth and Nicholas, whom Nadine has raised with loving guidance from her mother Mary and Grandmother Rahan. Michael became a successful businessman, lived overseas running companies, and returned to marry Ani Pehlivanian. Michael and Ani were blessed with two children, Ardem Haig and Taline Josephine. Michael too, was touched in many ways by Rahan's loving force.

Mgrditch and Rahan's youngest child, Mardig, inherited his father's creativity. He paints, sculpts and went on to teach his craft at Queens College. He found his niche in developing and renovating New York City real estate. Mardig, like his father, loves the planning and execution involved with construction. Mardig has long ago given up his loft studio on West Street in downtown Manhattan, but still maintains his residence in a building he owns in Tribeca. He continues with his art projects in his building in Brooklyn.

But I seem to be getting ahead of Rahan's tale. Back on Sedgwick Avenue in the Bronx, Rahan made another move. In 1974, Rahan negotiated the sale of the house she had shared with so much love with her beloved husband, Mgrditch, his parents Garabed and Kohar and with her three children. Rahan moved in with Krikor and Berjouhi at their home in Yonkers, New York and lived with them for ten years. In 1984, Rahan made another decisive move. This time she opted for independence and the rekindling of old relationships. Rahan moved from Yonkers to Leonia, New Jersey. The location was perfect. She lived in the midst of many of her old friends, and only minutes away to her church and senior citizen meeting hall.

Rahan passed many happy years in her new abode with a clutch of dear friends. She enjoyed time with Mr. and Mrs. Souren Choolfaian, Mr. and Mrs. Papazian, Mrs. Mirakian, Mrs. Tufankjian, and Mrs. Satenig Catchouny during these years. During this period, from the middle 1980's to the middle 1990's, sadly, many of Rahan's friends (and fellow survivors) passed away. So, in 1994, Rahan moved in with my wife Mary and me in Oradell, New Jersey. Rahan made it clear that she would be an equal contributor to our home. Immediately she assumed the roles of chef, domestic engineer and governor of the gardens. There was no responsibility or task she would shirk.

During the next ten years with us, Rahan also became a spokesperson for all victims of the Armenian Genocide. She was featured in a documentary about the Genocide produced and aired by the BBC, she appeared on PBS, NJ News 12, CBS Radio and in the "Bergen Record." Her videotaped story can be found on such websites as The Forgotten.com and TwentyVoices.com. In 2005, the Prelacy of the Armenian Apostolic Church of America honored Rahan as "Mother of the Year."

Sorrowfully, one year after she was named "Mother of the Year", our Prelate, Oshagan Surpazan, eulogized Rahan at her wake. He told her, "Mayrig (mother): you can rest now. Your job here on earth is done. You have raised your family well and you can be proud." On February 20, 2006, Rahan Delerian Kachian rejoined her beloved Mgrditch. She had lived through hell, went on to have a full life, and at last, could rest in peace.

Chapter 43

A Final Look Back

I was comfortably seated in the spacious, high-ceilinged clubhouse which adjoined my daughter and son-in-law's Studio City California complex. It was a bright, sunny January day in 1999. My wife Mary and I had travelled to Los Angeles from our home in New Jersey to await the birth of our first grandchild into the family. After he finely made his appearance Mary and I, like all new grandparents, were "popping our buttons" in pride. The happy Mom and Dad, Nadine and Greg cuddled and cooed their precious package and named him John Gregor. John Gregor Koobatian, the first of the second generation of my bloodline. Mary and I into Nadine and now Nadine and Greg into John. Praise God!

I suppose I was in a contemplative, perhaps even nostalgic mood. I was grateful for the blessings of life, fulfilled and deeply contented. I was also absorbed with visions of my past, dreams of the future, and of course, the glow of the moment. Silently I gave thanks for the safe arrival of a continued generation. My essence of all I was and of all that went before me was strengthened, reinforced, restructured and reborn. What a miracle. I know it's been said countless times before, but what a miracle!

It was here in California when I resolved to finally pen my ancestry. The history of the Sarajians and Sergenians. As I have noted much earlier in this narrative, it was my sister Mary who more than twenty years earlier had coaxed our mother to uncover the shrouded chronicles of her and our father's past lives. Ardemis Sergenian Sarajian gave to my sister a concentrated account of her family history, fully and willingly. For some reason Ardemis was no longer determined to guard and conceal her nightmares from the past.

As the years passed we grew older and with the Grace of God our families prospered. But in the cycle of life we also suffered the casualties of time. Mgrditch Kachian (Mary's father) died in 1964 a young sixty-two leaving behind his wife Rahan, age 53, and never having seen any of his grandchildren. That started a sad cavalcade of family deaths. After Avedis' passing in 1967, most of our uncles and aunts also died. The loss of Uncle Kaloust was especially painful as was the premature passing of his daughter Araxy. She was my closest contemporary. We were born only months apart and I always shared a special kinship with her.

Dick and I acted as pallbearers at our Godfather's funeral in Detroit as sister Mary looked on. Hagop Nergizian was a gentle benevolent man who was much respected and loved by Avedis and the entire family. We wept when Yeghishe Catchouny left us, an Armenian scholar, patriot and hero. It took three more decades before his life's partner Satenig departed. But sadly their son Armen, grandson Tom and granddaughter Susan all died too soon, too early. Dick, Mary and I all circled and prayed with Hayr Nareg when our beloved mother Ardemis joined her life's mate "Baron Avedis" in 1992. My cousin Souren's death which followed did not come as a complete shock, but more as a great loss. He had so much to give. I don't believe any of us could feel the heartbreak that Dick endured. Dick and Sam were only cousins, but in its truest sense, they were "blood brothers."

The family also grieved with deep emotion at the loss of our devoted clergy. The passing of our spiritual beacon, Archbishop Mesrop Ashjian, assailed all who knew him. He was the epitome of a man who was a giant and still wore the cloak of humility. He was everyone's friend. He was "The Beloved Surpazan." In Surpazan's last visit to our home in November of 2003, I "captured" him in a photo with Dick and Mom Rahan Kachian. For sure, I can "picture" all three, together now.

Dick and I, along with our entire family were totally shaken at the unexpected loss of our "family angel" our hokis sister Mary in 2001. The disaster of "9/11" was not the only tragedy we endured that year.

When we lost Mom Kachian it was as if another tower, or better said, a temple, had toppled. Rahan was such a vital, powerful and endearing pillar of love and strength that the void left by her loss keeps us searching for her presence. Often we talk as if she was still with us. In many ways, she still is.

Then, in July of 2006 my core was shaken and my heart again broken. My dearest hokis brother drew his final earthly breath and joined the spirits of all our departed. Dick was eighty three years old, and I have heard and know the oft used cliché that he enjoyed a full life. I am also thankful that Dick was now free from the wracking physical pains he endured during the past decade. But for me at least, parting was not sweet sorrow. It is a terrible ache. I used the word "hokis" brother, but please understand that I use that word with care and loving tenderness for it was <u>his</u> word, used frequently and always with affection.

Then, a short while ago in California, we were pained by the unexpected death of our sweet songstress Arouse Dermengian Devenish. She died just weeks after Dick. Each and every death has pierced our hearts and has chipped at the bark of our family tree. Every wound has made me realize that we are all transients and susceptible to the inevitable. I guess the message is as simple as it is old. Cherish life, yours and others. It is fragile, temporary and irreplaceable. It is said that its true worth can only be measured by its loss.

Since I was assigned this role as a narrator of my parents' saga, much has come to pass. Now ten years later, I feel the need to finally rest the pen and conclude the story. I know that the hands of time will write on, but my own efforts have been completed.

The Silent Generation

Epilogue

Compiling and writing this family history has taken me more than ten years. I have endeavored to remember with honor those members of my family who have passed on to a better place.

They will all be remembered. True, we still shed tears, for they are the evidence and testimony to each other, that we loved them so.

I will conclude the final page of this work with a poem, which was read, as requested by my sister Mary, at her wake. I believe it touches the essence of what Mary was. Her giving spirit and her deep sensitivity for others is the unmistakable message why she chose this piece to be shared with all those she loved. If it were not for Mary, most of this history would not exist. For it was Mary who coaxed these stories out of my mother and documented this information that I can now share with you.

To Those I Love
by Isla P. Richardson
If I should ever leave you
Whom I love
To go along the Silent Way,
Grieve not,
Nor speak of me with tears,
But laugh and talk
Of me as if I were

Beside you there.
(I'd come-I'd come, could I but find away!
But would not the tears and grief
Be barriers?)
And when you hear a song
Or see a bird
I loved, please do not let
the thought of me
Be sad… For I am
loving you just as
I always have…
You were so good to me!
There are so many things
I wanted still
To do- so many things
To say to you…
Remember that I
Did not fear…It was
Just leaving you
that was so hard to face…
We cannot see Beyond…
But this I know:
I loved you all so- 'twas heaven
Here with you!

<u>Acknowledgments</u>

With deep gratitude, I thank my wife Mary for her many hours of translating my hand written text into discernible words on the keyboard and computer. You worked wonders, Mary.

To Nadine Koobatian whose tireless energy in editing and re-editing, graphic design and production made this book possible. There are "thinkers" and there are "doers." Nadine is the perfect combination of the two.

To my daughter Nadine (yes, the same) and her husband Greg and to my son Michael and his wife Ani for their boundless interest and support and most of all for their love with has always sustained us, their parents.

To my nephew Kenneth Sarajian and all the family of my brother Dick, my heartfelt thanks for their caring and guidance to help me complete this family project. I also thank many of our relatives and friends who spent hours reading drafts of these stories and offering opinions.

Of course, none of the considerable effort put forth by Mary, Nadine, Ken or my friends, would have borne results had it not been for my sister Mary. It was Mary who with her gentle and sensitive persuasion exposed the hidden life that had dwelt in the reclusive recesses of my mother's mind. Together, mother and daughter, Ardemis and Mary, explored the long gone past and gave to the rest of us our own niche in the cosmos. We know now, at least, in part from where we came.

Finally, but not lastly, I must add that while it was the sacrifices of the Survivors that prodded me on to complete this book, it was my grandchildren who supplied the fuel. What grace was gained by the valor of our ancestor's deeds if their legacy was not harvested by their heirs? It is John, Elizabeth, Nicholas, Ardem and Taline, our grandchildren, who are the chosen to fulfill the promise and dreams of our slain and exiled generation. It is always the next generation, the children, who are our hope.

This has been a long journey for me. The total package has taken me more than ten years to compile, arrange and complete. It has been an emotional privilege to revisit the lives of Avedis and Ardemis and their Khnamies. I am proud of what we have preserved.

Geneology

The Branches of Our Ancestry

Part I- Sarajian
Assadour Sarajian
   b. 1830s (?), Efkere
   m. 1860s (?) to <u>Goulana Keosaian</u>
   d. Date unknown, Efkere (?)
   Brothers and Sisters: (?)

    Assadour Sarajian Married to Goulan Keosaian

Goulana Keosaian
   b. 1840s (?) Efkere
   m. 1860s(?) to <u>Assadour Sarajian</u>
   d. Date unknown, Efkere (?)
   Brothers and Sisters: (?)
   Children: Dikran and (?)

Children of the union of Assadour and Goulana Sarajian

      Dikran Sarajian
      b. 1860s, Efkere
      m. 1880s to <u>Mariam Kaloostian</u>
      d. 1915, Efkere
      Children: Markouhi, Minas and Avedis

Kaloostian
Mgrditch Kaloostian
b. 1830s, Nize
m. 1860s to Egisabet Kedarian
d. Date unknown, Nize
Brothers and Sisters: (?)

    Mgrditch Kaloostian Married to Egisabet Kedarian

Egisabet Kedarian
b. 1840s, Place (?)
m. 1860s to Mgrditch Kaloostian
d. Date and place unknown

The Silent Generation

Brothers and Sisters: (?)
Children: Jevan, Name Unknown Male, Mariam

Jevan Kaloostian
b. 1860s, Nize
m. (?)
d. unknown

Name Unknown Male Kaloostian
b. 1860s, Nize
m. (?)
d. 1915, Constantinople
Children: At least 2

Mariam Kaloostian
b. late 1860s, Nize
m. 1880s to Dikran Sarajian
d. 1915, Efkere
Children: Markouhi, Minas and Avedis

Children of the union of Dikran and Mariam Kaloostian Sarajian

Markouhi Sarajian Kalashian
b. 1880s, Efkere
m. 1890s to (?) Kalashian, Efkere
d. 1915, Efkere with her husband and all 5 children

Minas Sarajian
b. 1880s, Efkere
m. Early 1900s, Efkere
d. 1915, Efkere with his wife and their two children

Avedis (John) Sarajian
b. October 16, 1890, Efkere
m. first marriage to Vartouhi (died 1915, Efkere)
Child: Mariam (born 1914, Efkere, died 1915, Efkere)
m. second marriage to Ardemis Sergenian on October 16, 1921, NYC, USA
Children: Dikran, Mariam, Haig
d. January 6, 1967, NYC, USA

Avedis Sarajian Married to Ardemis Sergenian

The Silent Generation

Ardemis (Anna) Sergenian Sarajian
b. May 15, 1902, Shabin Karahisar
m. first marriage to Hamazasp Balian (b. 1897, Tamzara, d. 1915), Tamzara
m. second marriage to Avedis Sarajian, October 16, 1921
d. January 2, 1992, Teaneck, NJ
Brothers and Sisters: Victoria, Andon, Khosrophitookht, Kaloust and Souren
Children: Dikran, Mariam, Souren, Haig

Children of the Union of Avedis and Ardemis Sergenian Sarajian

Dikran (Dick) Sarajian
b. August 19, 1922, Brooklyn, NY
m. 1950 to Arax Catchouny, NY (born 1928 to Yeghishe and Satenig and Sister to Alice and Armen.)
Children: Richard, Kenneth and Carol

Children of the Union of Dick and Arax Catchouny Sarajian

Richard Sarajian
b. 1951, NJ
m. to Nora Daghlian, 1987 (born in 1958 to Reverend and Yeretzgin Daghlian and sister to Sonya, John, Aida and Houry)
Children: Ara (1988), Raffi (1991), Garo (1992) and Haig (1996)

Kenneth Sarajian
b. 1953, NJ
m. to Patricia Driemeyer, 1991 (born in 1957 to Douglas and Elizabeth Driemeyer and sister to Doug and Betsy)
Children: Ani (1993) and Stephen (1994)

Carol Sarajian Kennelly
b. 1957, NJ
m. to James Kennelly (born in 1957 to Joe and Elaine Kennelly and brother to Joseph, Marion, and Mary Jane)
Children: Michael (1989) and Daniel (1992)

Mariam ("Mary") Sarajian

329

b. April 19, 1924, NY
d. August 5, 2001, NJ

Souren ("Sourig") Sarajian
b. October 19, 1928, NY
d. April 1929, NY

Haig ("Haigy") Sarajian
b. October 16, 1930, NY
m. to Mary Kachian (born in 1932, NY, daughter to Mgrditch and Rahan Kachian and sister to Berjouhi and Mardig)
Children: Nadine (1965) and Michael (1966)

Children of the Union of Haig and Mary Kachian Sarajian

> Nadine Sarajian Koobatian
> b. 1965, NY
> m. 1997, NJ to Gregor Koobatian of Worcester, MA, son of John and Rose Koobatian and brother to Tom, Carol and Paul
> Children: John, (1999, California), Elizabeth (2001, Connecticut) and Nicholas (2003, Connecticut)

> Michael S. Sarajian
> b. 1966, NY
> m. in 2004 in NJ to Ani Pehlivanian, daughter of John and Joanne Pehlivanian and sister to Mari and Aram, NJ
> Children: Ardem Haig (2007) and Taline Josephine (2008)

Part II- Sergenian
Mgrditch Sergenian
b. 1840s, Shabin Karahisar
m. 1860s to Seranoush (?)
d. (?)
Children: Only one known child: Sarkis Sergenian

Mgrditch Sergenian Married to Seranoush Sergenian

The Silent Generation

Seranoush Sergenian
b. 1840s, Shabin Karahisar
d. (?)
Children: Sarkis Sergenian

Child born from the union of Mgrditch and Seranoush Sergenian

Sarkis Sergenian
b. late 1860s, Shabin Karahisar
m. about 1890 to Anna Papazian, Shabin Karahisar
d. 1907, Shabin Karahisar
Children: Victoria, Andon, Khosrophitookht (Aghavni), Kaloust, Ardemis, Souren.

Papazian
Mgrditch Papazian
b. 1840, Tokat
m. first marriage (1860s) to Name Unknown, b. 1870(?). d. (?), Jerusalem
Children with first wife: Dikran (1866?), Hripsimeh (?), Anna (1870?), Dourig (1872?), Haiganoush (1874?)
m. second marriage to Nazeli Ozanian, b. mid or late 1870s, Shabin Karahisar, d. 1920 (?), Varna, Bulgaria, sister to Antranik Ozanian.
Children with second wife: Mariam (1880s), Armenouhi (1880s) and Yervant (1880s).

Children of the Union of Mgrditch and First Wife Papazian

Dikran Papazian
b. 1860s, Tokat
m. 1890s, Tokat (?)
Children: Yervant
d. Unknown

Hripsimeh Papazian Odabashian
b. 1860s, Tokat
m. 1890s to (?) Odabashian
Children: Unknown
D: 1915, Shabin Karahisar

Anna Papazian Sergenian
b. 1870s(?), Tokat
m. 1890 to Sarkis Sergenian in Shabin Karahisar

Children: Victoria (1891), Andon (1894), Khosrophitookht (Aghavni) (1896), Kaloust (1899), Ardemis (1902), and Souren (1904)
d. 1912, Tokat

Dourig Papazian
b. 1872, Tokat
m. 1890s to (?)
Children: (?)
d. 1915, Shabin Karahisar

Haiganoush Papazian Mozian
b. 1874 (?), Tokat
m. 1890s to (?) Mozian
Children: At least one, Seranoush, who later married Hamazasp Agababian, who was the uncle (father's brother) of Keghanoush, wife of Kaloust Sergenian and the mother of Haig and Edward Agababian.)
d. 1915, Shabin Karahisar

Children of the Union of Mgrditch Papazian and Nazeli Ozanian

Mariam Papazian
b. 1880s, Shabin Karahisar
m. Unknown
d. date unknown, Paris, France

Armenouhi Papazian Kelerchian
b. 1880s, Shabin Karahisar
m. 1900s, to (?) Kelerchian
d. date unknown, Paris, France

Yervant Papazian
b. 1880s, Shabin Karahisar
m. 1915 (?) in Georgia
d. date unknown

Children of the Union of Sarkis and Anna Papazian Sergenian

Victoria Sergenian Durgerian
b. 1891, Shabin Karahisar

m. 1909 to (?) Durgerian, Shabin Karahisar.
Husband was born late in 1880s in Shabin
Karahisar and died in 1915 in Karahisar

Andon Sardjenian (he changed the spelling)
b. 1894, Shabin Karahisar
m. 1923, Athens, Greece to Shoushan Shahinian
(also spelled Chahinian) (born in 1904 in Van,
Turkey, d. 1998, California)

Khosrophitookht (Aghavni or Mary) Sergenian
Dermengian
b. 1896, Shabin Karahisar
m. first husband, 1913, Tokat (he died in 1915)
m. second husband, Mirijan ("Mike")
Dermengian, 1921, Syracuse, NY, (he was born
in 1881, Sepastia, youngest of 13 children,
married first wife in Sepastia in late 1890s and
had six children. His first wife and six children
were all killed in 1915. He died in 1972,
California)
Children: (Aghavni and Mirijan): Souren (1922-
1993), Arouse (1925-2008)
Grandchildren: Diane and John, Paul and Ani

Kaloust ("George") Sergenian
b. 1899, Shabin Karahisar
m. 1926 in Massachusetts to Keghanoush
Agababian (born in 1926 in Papert, Turkey.
One of thirteen children. Died 1995 in
Massachusetts)
Children: Keghvart ("Kay") (1927), Arax
(1931-1990), Anahid (1935), and Sona (1944)
Grandchildren: Charles and Karen, Zaven and
Nina, Peter, Daniel and Christina, Michael,
Robin, Ruth and Sarah
Great-grandchildren: Twelve
d. 1983, Massachusetts

Ardemis ("Anna") Sergenian Sarajian
b. May 15, 1902, Shabin Karahisar
m. first marriage to Hamazasp Balian, Tamzara,
1915. He died in 1915.

m. second marriage to <u>Avedis Sarajian</u>, 1921.
Avedis died in 1967, NY
Children: Dikran (1922), Mariam (1926-2001),
Souren (1928-1929), and Haig (1930)
Grandchildren: Richard, Kenneth, Carol,
Nadine and Michael
Great-grandchildren: Ara, Raffi, Garo, Haig,
Ani, Stephen, Michael, Daniel, John, Elizabeth,
Nicholas, Ardem and Taline
d. 1992, Teaneck, NJ

<u>Souren Sergenian</u>
b. 1904, Shabin Karahisar
d. 1915, Tokat (?)

Sources

[1] Dadrian, Vahakn N., <u>Warrant for Genocide, Key Elements of the Turko-Armenian Conflict</u>, 1999, p. 123 (quoting Turkish Governor-General Nazim's declaration that the extermination of the Armenians was meant to "solve the Eastern Question. (hall edecek)", Takvimi Vekayi, no. 3540, p.8.

[2] This information was obtained from Mary Sarajian, the widow of Assadour Sarajian, a cousin living in Watertown, Massachusetts.

[3] Chalabian, Antranig, <u>General Antranik and the Armenian Revolutionary Movement</u>, 1988, p. 290.

[4] <u>Id</u>. Antranik had also attained high military rank in Bulgaria and was honored there as he was by his own Nation.

[5] <u>Id.</u>

[6] <u>Id</u>. at 538.

[7] <u>Id</u>.

[8] <u>Id</u>.

[9] It was interesting that my great-grandfather's second wife, Nazeli, had a part in Antranik's marriage to Nevart. Antranik had been married to a young woman in Shabin Karahisar. Sadly he lost both his first wife and baby in childbirth after just one year of marriage. Henceforth, he had been married to his people's quest for freedom. Once in Bulgaria, however, Nazeli met Nevart, a young, attractive, and intelligent Armenian girl. Antranik and Nevart exchanged photos and soon after were wed. A few months after the wedding, the couple traveled to America. They arrived in New York City on July 12, 1922, but eventually settled in Fresno, California.

[10] Chalabian, p. 541-42.

---

[11] Haigaz, Aram, The Fall of the Aerie, (undated), p. 56-59.

[12] Papazian, Michael, B. Light from Light, 2006, p. 164.

[13] Toynbee, Arnold, J., Armenian Atrocities, The Murder of a Nation, 1975, p. 18, from a speech delivered by Lord Bryce to the British House of Lords, October 6, 1915.

[14] Id.

[15] Morgenthau, Henry, Ambassador Morgenthau's Story, republished in 2000, pp. 192-93, (Between 1895-96, "nearly 200,000 Armenians were most atrociously done to death. But through all these years, the existence of the Armenians was one continuous nightmare. Their property was stolen, their men were murdered, their women were ravished, their young girls were kidnapped and forced to live in Turkish harems.")

[16] Morgenthau, p. 205-06.

[17] Id. at 204-06.

[18] Id. ("The Turks never had the slightest idea of reestablishing the Armenians in this new country. They knew that the great majority would never reach their destination and that those who did would either die of thirst or starvation, or be murdered by the wild Mohammedan desert tribes...When Turkish authorities gave the orders for these deportations, they were merely giving a death warrant to the whole race; they understood this well, and, in their conversations with me, they made no particular attempt to conceal the fact.")

[19] Morgenthau, p. 201, ("in many instances, Armenian soldiers [fighting for the Turks in the Turkish army] were disposed of in even more summary fashion, for it now became almost the general practice to shoot them in cold blood.")

[20] Id. at 209.

---

[21] Id at 210.

[22] Id.

[23] Sometime during his service with the Antranik Volunteer Brigade, Andon found himself in Russia (or perhaps Georgia) and was befriended by a young Communist revolutionary. His name was Anastas Mikoyan, himself later a butcher of Armenians (in Soviet Armenia) and intimate cohort of Joseph Stalin.

[25] Much of the information on Arabgir was found in the excellent book, Arabgir- the History, by George Jerjian.

[26] According to Dr. Robert Hewsen's Historical Atlas, Arabgir was one of those towns in Anatolia where the majority of local men "left" their homes, wives and children and sought work elsewhere." Robert Hewsen, Historical Atlas of Armenia, p. 197. This indicates, (to me at least) that the women and children did much of the farming and the manufacturing of the cotton products. Professor Hewsen also writes that the American Board of Protestant Churches founded and maintained an active mission in Arabgir in 1853. Dr. Hewsen notes that at the dawn of the Twentieth Century Arabgir had become the hub of Catholicism in Anatolia. It is interesting, but perhaps a study for another time, that here in the heartland of an Islamic state, both the Catholic and Protestant Churches were unable in their evangelical fervor to convert the Moslems to Christianity. Instead they concentrated on recruiting Armenian Apostolics to fulfill their missionary obligations. Fortunately, after 1915 their efforts were refocused on saving the orphaned children of the massacred Armenians.

[27] As we explore the life of Der Hoosig and his family I relied on various reference sources. Most of the Catchouny historical and biographical data came to me from personal notes and conversations with Kenneth Sarajian, Arax Sarajian and Alice Hagopian. I derived additional facts from Yeghishe's own words in his historical memoirs, Travels with Antranik. The fullest find of information I garnered was from the videotape so thoughtfully made of Satenig Catchouny by Ken Sarajian shortly before her death.

While compiling all my sources, Richard Sarajian (grandson of Yeghishe and Satenig) provided me with a book that answered many of my queries. Richie's stern reminder to me was "if you are going *to write about my great grandfather Der Hoosig, you might as well be accurate.*" Gathering "accurate" facts about a legendary figure that lived more than one hundred years ago was no easy task. The reference book Richie shared with me was <u>Memory-Relic of the Genocide</u>, by E. Atamasian. Within its pages the author who was witness to the events reveals the circumstances surrounding the final months and ultimate death of Der Hoosig Catchouny. It is a stirring disclosure, vividly portraying one of the first organized "death marches" out of Constantinople and destined for the deserts of Der Zor in Syria.

[28] Atamasian, E. <u>Memory-Relic of the Genocide.</u>

[29] Hewsen, Robert, <u>Armenia: A Historical Atlas</u>, p. 23.

[30] Much of my information on Aghtamar was gleamed from the following publication, <u>Aghtamar, The Church of the Holy Cross, 915-921</u>, AGBU, Alex Manoogian Cultural Fund.

[31] I strongly recommend family members borrow these priceless documents for a taste of our history. They are available in English from Arax Sarajian. The Catchouny books are openly available but the treasured notes, papers, letters and other written material still lie in the guarded hands of the family.

[32] Haigaz, Aram, <u>The Fall of the Aerie</u>, p. 64

[33] The concluding segment of Yeghishe and Satenig's story is almost wholly transcribed by the papers and records given to me by Kenneth Sarajian.

.